Youth Ministry That Works

Practical Ideas for Working with Young People

GEORGE BORAN

PAULIST PRESS
New York / Mahwah, N.J.

Cover design by Herbert Herrera.

Library of Congress Cataloging-in-Publication Data

Boran, George, 1941–
    Youth ministry that works : practical ideas for working with young people / George Boran.
        p.   cm.
    Includes bibliographical references.
    ISBN 0-8091-3666-X (alk. paper)
    1. Church work with youth—Catholic Church. I. Title.
BX2347.8.Y7B67 1996
259'.23–dc20   96-23802
                                                                                      CIP

Published by Paulist Press
997 Macarthur Boulevard
Mahwah, New Jersey 07430

Printed and bound in the
United States of America

Contents

3. STAGES OF FAITH DEVELOPMENT
(Community and Social Model)

4. OTHER FACTORS

OBSERVATIONS

Foreword

With the publication of this book, a new voice address-ing youth ministry comes to be heard in North America, that of George Boran. Here we have a man of Ireland trained as a missionary, who served twenty-five years in Brazil both in pastoral ministry and in the administrative, organizational ministry of the National Youth Office of the Brazilian Roman Catholic Bishop's Conference, now speaking about youth ministry in North America.

What deserves to be highlighted about this book is something alluded to in its introduction but the significance of which could easily be overlooked. The book itself repre-sents important transitions—or better, transformations—in Boran's thinking. In the end the process that produced *Youth Ministry That Works* might be almost as illuminating and significant as its content.

When he arrived in the United States in 1993, Boran had in hand his already published books about youth ministry seen from a South American perspective. Written in Portuguese and Spanish, these works emerged originally from his presentations to youth leaders and other pastoral agents, chiefly, but not exclusively, in Brazil. Correctly, he sensed that his insights and proposals might be useful in North America. Wisely, he asked various youth ministry authors and leaders in the United States to review what he had done and to judge whether the materials were suitable for publication here. Patiently, he gathered what must have been a dizzying array of critiques from varied perspectives, some of them surely blind to their own assumptions. Very wisely, he decided to take two inconvenient steps. One was to do doctoral-level study that would verify or alter his ideas. The second was to rewrite his vision of youth ministry in the light of this deeper and more broadly focused study and in the light of the situation in North America.

Of course, this is not to say that youth ministry—and the church in general in North America—does not have much to learn from the church in South America, especially the one in Brazil. Though the influence of liberation theology has not been as great in the North American churches or in their ministry to youth as one would hope, that influence still has been decisive for the thinking of many. We in the United States have lessons yet to be learned from youth ministry done among desperately poor young people in Latin America. Most in North America are still unaware of the treasures to be found in the statements about young people of the Medellín, Puebla, and Santo Domingo documents. Here Boran gives us access to some of these lessons and statements.

Readers will do well to keep in mind George Boran's important South American background. Even more significant is to keep in mind that what he offers us here is not simply a translation of his earlier work. He walked a whole new walk in thinking through and writing this book.

These matters are laid out in his own introduction. Here, his judicious warnings about the too-narrow character of some approaches to youth ministry and the need for a more global vision are to some extent a verification of his own journey toward deeper foundations and a broader vision. The book itself is an invitation to youth workers to reconsider, the way he himself did, some of their assumptions about youth ministry theory and practice in a search for a deeper spirituality, a more critical awareness, more astute formation practices, and a long-term vision. Response to that invitation could inspire creative ferment in North American youth ministry. That is my hope for this book.

Michael Warren
St. John's University,
Jamaica, N.Y.
31 January 1996

Introduction

Once upon a time there was an Indian prince who invited a group of blind people to visit him in his palace. The prince placed the group in front of an elephant. Each was led by hand to a part of the elephant and asked to feel it. The prince then asked the blind people to explain what they thought was in front of them. The one that had felt the stomach said that it was a very large soft bag. The one with the tail disagreed, saying that it was a type of whip. The one who had felt the ears became angry and declared that it was a banana leaf. The one who touched the trunk mocked the others saying they were all wrong; it was a hose pipe. The one who explored the leg affirmed that it was a strong post-firmly set in the ground. The blind people then started quarrelling among themselves, each one claiming to be right. Each one believes that the whole must look like the piece he or she touches and that his or her understanding is the only correct one.

This is a well-known story that I sometimes tell to illustrate an important requirement for those who work with youth: leaders need a global vision of where they are going and how they hope to get there. Each blind person perceived a part of the elephant but was unable to understand the part as related to the whole.

In youth ministry something similar occurs. Youth leaders sometimes become excited with some aspect of methodology for youth ministry. Some, for example, may look upon relationships as the solution for pastoral problems. Others may put their faith in youth retreats. Or others yet may look upon the see-judge-act method as the salvation of youth ministry. People are disappointed when the desired results are not achieved. They fail to see their error. They have focused only on some of the parts of a wider process, and they have ignored the need for each part to be coordinated with others within a broader methodology. Relationships, youth retreats, the see-judge-act method, and other strategies should be seen as valuable strategies but not the totality of the solution. The different parts of youth methodology have to fit into one another to make youth ministry move forward. One cog spinning alone is ineffective in a powerful machine.

The Need for a Theory

A global vision presupposes a theory or philosophy of youth ministry that interlocks the different parts: sexuality, affection, relationships, spirituality, biblical formation, theological formation, critical awareness, action, formation through action, systematic follow-up, organizational structures, coordination committees, stages of faith development, the history of youth ministry, youth culture, social problems, models youth ministry, psychological factors in motivation, courses, seminars, encounters, retreats, assemblies, mass rallies, small group ministry, pastoral planning, and social commitment.

Process of Elaboration of This Book

When I took over as national youth minister for the Brazilian Bishops' Conference in 1984, I started writing this book. I had already written a number of successful books on youth ministry, but I wanted this one to be more comprehensive. The original plan proved to be impracticable. It was

does, the worse it seems to get. There is no doubt that external social and political circumstances place difficulties in the way, but I believe that the main obstacle is in ourselves." One young person observed: "Youth ministry, in many places, has learned the art of going around and around in circles without getting anywhere." The challenges are many: difficulty in forming new groups, lack of perseverance, lack of commitment, lack of capable and committed leaders, superficiality in meetings, improvising, lack of continuity, lack of spirituality, lack of critical awareness, lack of formation, lack of conversion, and absence of any long-term vision. The big question in the minds of many youth leaders is: "Where are we going wrong?" The answer to this question and the presentation of concrete solutions are what this book is about.

There has been a cultural change in recent years that has caught many youth leaders by surprise. The way of thinking of a young person today is different from that of a young person of the sixties, seventies, or eighties. We have to adapt our theory of youth ministry to a generation that is very different.

Goodwill is no longer sufficient for working with youth. Today we need also to be competent. This book does not, however, intend to give recipes. It is not a partitur from which the violinist plays. An effort has been made to avoid presenting prescriptions that may apply today and not tomorrow. Any theory must grow lest it die. Realities are very different. This work aims, rather, at giving the ingredients so that each can make her own recipe, according to the diversity of challenges and circumstances. A football player practices different strategies, but when he receives a ball in an unexpected way, he has to adapt his theory to meet a new situation. Some young people live in rural areas with difficulty in communication; others live in urban areas. In large cities there are other differences. Work in poor neighborhoods where the majority of young people are from disadvantaged sectors of the population is different from work in neighborhoods where most are from the middle class. Each group—as each person—is unique.

The theory of youth ministry described here presupposes investment of material and human resources. We do not present any magic formula that works without adequate tools. One young person commented: "I can be a good painter, but if you give me spoiled brushes, I can't paint a beautiful picture."

Different Ways of Using This Book

This book can be used in a variety of ways:

Personal reading opens up a global vision of youth ministry where different parts are integrated in a coherent whole. The book can serve as a reference for preparing talks and courses, for doing evaluations, or for finding solutions to immediate difficulties. As a reference book it can indicate pitfalls. One young person observed: "Is it really necessary for youth leaders to take the path that has the most chasms and quicksands—where many disappear? With proper guidance we could take more efficacious ways."

This book can be studied in **weekly meetings** of youth groups. Questions and activities have been placed at the end of each chapter for this purpose. One enthusiastic group spent a week in a beach house studying a previous book. Four hours each day were dedicated to study, and the rest to leisure. Many creative solutions are possible!

My concern in writing this book was to present ideas and suggestions that work. I tried to avoid theoretical expositions that have internal logical coherence but do not work in practice. I thank the thousands of young people and adult youth ministers who participated with me in meetings, courses, and assemblies of evaluation and planning, and whose ideas and intuitions appear throughout this work. After finishing the Portuguese and Spanish versions of this book, I moved to the United States to pursue graduate studies in the area of leadership and youth. As I started the English translation and the adaptation to a First World context, I was fortunate to receive help from very capable people with experience in youth ministry in the United States, England, and Ireland: Professors John Nelson and Gloria Durka at Fordham University; authors Michael Warren and John Roberto; experienced youth ministers Debby Farwell, John Nevins, Jim Morgan, and Eamon Mulcahy. I wish to thank especially Michael McCarthy, youth minster for the Rockville Centre diocese, Long Island, New York, who accompanied me through the different stages of adaptation to a First World context and offered valuable suggestions. My own work with youth ministry in the same diocese was an important part of the adaptation process.

Although this book was prepared as an aid for those who work in youth ministry, the basic principles are the same for all ministries. People who work with married couples, preparation for confirmation, religious instruction, Christian base communities, and social work will find many useful hints to improve the efficacy of their work in these pages.

We are fortunate to be living at a moment in history when gigantic transformations are taking place. Our sincerest wish is that, as church, we will not miss the train of history once again. There is still time. Our ability to work with young people will be the litmus test of our capacity to move into a new era. We hope this book will help those who believe in young people and are searching for more efficacious ways of reaching them with the inspiring message of the Christian faith.

Pastoral work with young people is a critical issue for

the church today. This stage in life represents the greatest concentration of physical, psychological, emotional, and intellectual growth for a human being. It is a time when people are most open to formation and to taking decisive steps that can determine future life direction. As people grow older, change becomes more difficult. This is also a privileged period for forming Christian leaders, leaders who can renew the church, society, and modern culture. Nothing could be more important than the formation of a new generation of youth leaders! At the end of one millennium and the beginning of another, we are being challenged to influence the religious education of a generation to build "a new heaven and a new earth" (Rev 21:1). We need the patience now to plant a sapling so that one day it may grow into a great tree. If we fail, there may not be another opportunity.

George Boran, C.S.Sp.

Characteristics of a New Model of Youth Ministry

Here Lies the Traditional Model

Failure of the Traditional Model

One thing is clear today. Parish structures, Catholic schools, religious education class, the family, and Sunday mass no longer have the same capacity to transmit the faith as before. With the change of the cultural background that sustained a traditional faith, the older formation methods are rapidly losing their ability to attract young people.

It is also clear that we cannot be prisoners of immediate results. We need to rethink more radically and more globally new forms for evangelizing youth. Religious education classes, Catholic school and Sunday mass are now seen as limited solutions. Catechetical programs that presuppose that age is the criterion for evaluating young people's faith development have to be questioned. More decisive factors can no longer be ignored. We need to have courage to deal with a central question: "Do we try to adapt young people to our programs or do we adapt our programs to young people?" This is a disturbing question for those who feel threatened by a new inductive methodology for which they were not prepared. It is in this context and to answer these challenges that a new approach to youth work emerges.

Birth of a New Model

For each age, the church elaborates a model for evangelizing youth. Vatican II talks about the need to read the "signs of the times." Models that worked in the past are frequently ineffective in terms of today's needs.

On different trips I have made in Latin America, Africa, Europe and the United States to speak on youth work, the emergence of this new model of ministry to youth has become apparent to me. There are different levels and stages of youth ministry. While some places are still beginning, others have advanced further down the road to a more committed ministry. Yet all are moving in the same direction. Despite differences between developed and developing countries, this model emerges with characteristics that are common. I believe the international aspect is important. We can help and learn from each other; we can share our experiences and discoveries; we can avoid the weakening effects of "inbreeding."

When we talk here about a new model, we are not proposing a complete rupture with what we are already doing. Rather, this new model aims at organizing what we are doing, so that we can see the bigger picture. It confirms us in the steps we have already taken. At the same time, this "new proposal" reveals new worlds to be conquered, new areas where we need to be challenged. It presents a road map of a more serious and challenging youth ministry for those who continue to have the courage to dream dreams. An understanding of the bigger picture can be important for evaluating progress and perceiving levels yet to be attained.

We now have the opportunity to avoid a type of religious education that forms young people with infantile attitudes, narrow horizons, and tunnel vision. A new model will be in tune with the generosity and idealism of young people and offer them "high and noble ideals that are inspired by their aspirations of a more just and fraternal society."[1]

INITIAL OBSERVATIONS

1. Characteristics of This Model

a. Clarity of Goals. "It's easy to organize outings for youth, bring together prayer groups, sponsor dances. The difficult challenge is to propose convincing Christian ideals that will give direction to their energies during a lifetime."[2] The new model, which we will describe presently, helps to clarify goals. Goals decide the direction we take. Without clear goals, we are shooting in the dark; precious energy and resources are consumed without getting anywhere. One young person complained: "My group spins and spins, always ending up in the same position."

The story is told of a man who accepted the challenge to run from his native village to the capital city and break an existing record. He bought special running shoes and trained daily; he went on a very strict diet; he dedicated himself to his all-consuming ambition. People admired his determination and will-power. The event was a continuous subject of conversation in the village. On the day of the race a crowd gathered to cheer him. They were proud of their champion. He ran well. He finished exhausted. There was only one problem: he took the wrong road and arrived in the wrong city.

Youth workers must first clarify their own goals—both conscious and unconscious—with a view to changing or improving them. Otherwise they are going to set out on a journey that has no clear destination. As youth leaders we need to clarify where we are going. Goals can be very narrow and superficial. One leader of a youth encounter movement explained: "The only thing that brings the members of my group together is the hope of being selected to work in our weekend encounters and experience the same emotion again." Goals can also be more demanding and liberating. One group worked for the renewal of church and society, motivated by the evangelical option for the poor. The first step in improving our goals is becoming aware of the real goals that are pointing us in a set direction.

A theory of youth ministry will indicate the correct goal (vision), which in turn will indicate the correct road to be taken (methodology). The temptation here is to invite in an expert to give a talk on the theory of youth ministry to **beginners** to get them to move faster. The faith journey, however, is not so simple. To do so would be to fall into the trap of the traditional deductive model of evangelization. Beginners do not begin by studying theory. Goals have to be discovered. At the beginning, each member of the group has his own goals and expectations. There is as yet no common goal. Goals are discovered under expert guidance. Gradually individual goals are modified and a group goal emerges. However, someone in the group—normally the youth leader or youth minister—needs to have the clarity that comes from an explicit theory; otherwise the blind will be leading the blind and "both will fall into the same ditch" (Lk 6:39). Many groups are in crisis because youth leaders have no clear theory of youth ministry, and therefore no clear goals and no clear direction.

b. Non-Formal Education This new model of youth ministry, however, uses a different methodology from that of *formal education* used in schools. Until recently, schools were almost the only model for educating youth in the faith. However, when we move to the parish community, to parish youth groups, or even to youth groups within the school itself, the same conditions for the functioning of the school model of formal education are no longer present: paid teachers, textbook, role call, punishment for constant absence, discipline, class atmosphere, daily contact with young people, annual curriculum implemented in chronological sequence, regular attendance motivated by pressure from parents, and the need to pass exams and prepare for a suitable career.

The difficulties of many youth ministers come from a lack of understanding of this change of pedagogical approach. The methodology in pastoral ministry is different: it is a process of **non-formal education**. Many advisers have been trained to work in a **formal educational** setting, in an institutional way or within institutions (schools, universities, seminaries, hospitals, social institutions), and have difficulty in adapting to the new rules of a non-formal situation. They are competent when it comes to giving a talk, a class, organizing from the top down. But in youth ministry they have difficulty in understanding that the rules, the attitudes and the methods now have to be different. In a school situation, teachers can count on the continuous presence of their pupils. In a community situation, on the other hand, youth ministers or youth leaders do not have a captive audience. They must motivate young people to come to the first meeting. After the first meeting the young people must be motivated to return to the next one. And so such is the case for every meeting. When meetings become tiring, repetitive and mediocre, young people cease to come. Youth ministry does not have guaranteed clients, and so, to be successful, it needs a high capacity of adaptation. It faces two options: adapt and respond to young people's needs or close down.

The deductive method of giving a class functions well in a school situation, but not in youth ministry. In a non-formal situation we need to use the **inductive method** that starts with the young person's life. This is how Jesus worked. The story of the disciples on the way to Emmaus depicts his method. Jesus does not start by giving them a lecture. Rather he starts patiently with their situation of discouragement and disillusionment to awaken them to faith in the resurrection. It was only at the end of the journey that his listeners recognized him, in the breaking of bread. In the same way, young people come together and reflect in small groups on their lives and experiences, inspired by their Christian faith.

Non-formal education is not limited to parishes. We can also use the method of non-formal education within the school environment, to the extent that we work with voluntary small groups outside a classroom situation. Within a school environment, therefore, both types of education can co-exist: formal and non-formal.

2. Observations on the Evangelization of Youth

It is important to be clear on the specific role of religious education in order not to reduce youth ministry to a movement to help others, a psychological clinic, or a political movement. While it is true that the evangelization of the young person must involve all the dimensions of his or her personality, nevertheless it cannot be reduced to one of these dimensions. The evangelizers of youth are aware that their mission is to proclaim the gospel to all creatures (Mk 16:15). Evangelization means bringing the gospel message to others. It means doing as Christ did. Evangelization constitutes the most profound identity of youth ministry. The evangelizer, as the sower, needs to prepare the ground, learn the best methods and the best time to plant. When the seeds begin to bud, he or she needs to water, manure, and accompany the new life that bursts forth.

Evangelization is a complex phenomenon that implies transformation, life witness, proclaiming Jesus Christ, adhesion to a concrete community, and participation in the mission of the church. Evangelization involves all the dimensions of the young person's life. That is why we speak of holistic formation.

Many young people still need to overcome an image of Christian faith as a belief in abstract doctrines unrelated to their daily lives. Faith is something much richer. It is a loving encounter with God who allows himself to be touched by us in the person of Jesus Christ.

Faith is a gift from God. "You have not chosen me, I have chosen you" (Jn 15:16). But faith also requires an option on our part. It is the freedom to be fully human and not the restriction of our humanity. Faith frees a power within us, a power that comes from God.

Conversion from "Received Faith" to "Owned Faith."

An important evolution in terms of conversion takes place as young people pass through different stages. Westerhoff speaks of conversion as a radical about-turn from "received faith" to "owned faith."[3]

Received Faith. This is the faith received through the environment where the young person lives: family and community. At this stage, people believe, largely, because of the influence and pressure of others. There is little personal decision. Unfortunately many Christians remain at this stage of "received faith," becoming "cultural Christians." In the past this type of faith was common to all, and for church structures this was the only mode of faith considered. A received faith, however, is no longer able to resist a changed environment. "Cultural Christians" wither under the strong heat of a new and pluralistic culture that questions even the most sacred beliefs.

But this is not a negative stage of faith. It only becomes negative when we become "stuck" and refuse to move on. So we can see this stage as a natural step in the evolution to adult faith. At this moment in the young person's life, sentiments and significant experiences are more important than intellectual reasons. The heart is more important than the head. Faith, in the final analysis, comes from God. God, nevertheless, works in an incarnate way, acting through human mediations. Each stage is built on a previous one; consequently, this initial stage must not be despised. It can serve as a foundation for a more complex and rooted faith later on. Many young people today do not have the foundation of "received faith" to build on. The family is disintegrating under the impact of the media and extreme poverty. Many parents are no longer practicing Christians. A youth group or encounter can, in fact, be the first contact of young people with the church. A significant number of youth have never talked to parish leaders or participated in a church community. This new phenomenon explains in part the increasing difficulty of youth ministry to involve youth in a conversion process.

Owned Faith. In "owned faith," young people take on responsibility for their own beliefs, actions and life style. This is a significant change from "received faith" that depended on the authority of the community. "Going along with the crowd" is "no longer in." It is no longer possible to hide in the group. The young person needs to look Jesus in the face and give a personal response to his invitation: "Come, follow me."

A more personal faith arises from the questioning and critical evolution of received faith. This can be a traumatic period for young people as they pass through a phase of questioning, doubts and conflict to arrive at personal convictions in regard to what is considered a worthwhile life. At this moment the "religion of the head" has the same importance as the "religion of the heart." Faith needs to be relevant socially. It is seen as the freedom to be fully human and not as something that confines our humanity. "Searching faith" is emphasized when religion of the head starts predominating over religion of the heart. The intellect starts to seek intellectual justification for faith. The person tries to discover convictions that are worth living and dying for.[4]

An understanding of this questioning phase is important for effective youth ministry. Unfortunately, some church leaders are unable to grasp the significance of this transition and reject young people for being critical of the church. A lack of understanding can abort the healthy transition of a young person to a stage of more mature faith.

The stage of "received faith" is important during early adolescence. This fact can question profoundly the methodology we use. Members of coordination committees are largely composed of young adults. Members of youth groups, on the other hand, are mainly adolescents. Coordination committees need, therefore, to reflect on concerns related to adolescence: To what extent are members considering the importance of the heart, of sentiments, and of significant experiences for adolescents at this age? To what extent are the older youth, members of the coordination committee, imposing more intellectual orientations, proper for their age bracket?

2

Stepping Stones in the Birth of This New Model

There are clearly defined steps in the emergence of this new model. Nevertheless, not all dioceses have taken the totality of the following steps.

1. Services to Youth

An initial step in building youth ministry has been the development of services to young people. Faced with the exodus of youth from the church, the limits of traditional methods, and the breakdown of the family as the privileged means of educating young people in the faith, many dioceses have taken an important step to reverse this tendency. Diocesan youth ministers are appointed to try out new ways of involving young people. The minister may be a priest, religious or lay adult who has a certain charisma for working with young people. This initial step has been the starting point for many new initiatives.

Thus a new type of ministry for youth emerges: a ministry that goes beyond the parish mass, the classroom and the family. Services are organized for young people, usually by adults. Many places organize youth centers, weekend courses, youth encounters, new style retreats, and youth rallies. Young people are contacted through parishes, schools or local organizations. Methods and content of these different approaches respond to the psychology of youth and are frequently a first step in awakening young people to a deeper understanding of the gospel message.

These initiatives have led to the creation of new and vital spaces for young people within the institutional church. These are autonomous spaces where young people live a model of church that is meaningful to them—where they can cultivate values they consider important, where they are treated as subjects rather than objects of their own educational process. This is one of the success stories of youth ministry. Most countries have already taken this first step.

2. Youth Groups

The formation of youth groups is a second level of the growth of youth ministry. Youth groups are a solution for two important challenges: the need for continuity and the influence of the peer group.

a. The Challenge of Continuity. Services to youth, on their own, have a serious flaw. They usually lack a plan for continuity. Youth encounters, retreats and rallies need to be part of a more ample response. On the following day, after an encounter, retreat or rally, the difficulty has to be faced: "And now that we have motivated the young people, what are we going to do with them?" What do we do when the young person returns to the individualistic and materialistic environment of society? What do we do when the individual returns to the secularized and non-supportive environment of the family? And what do we do when the young person returns to the cold and conservative environment of some parishes?

Alone the young person rarely has the strength to keep the flame of faith burning. Alone it is difficult to maintain an alternative life style—to swim against the current. An isolated young person is vulnerable and easily paralyzed by the surrounding environment. The previous level of services to youth has created sporadic opportunities of formation for youth within the church. Leaders now need to create permanent spaces where young people can cultivate alternative values and experience the support of others. Here one of the solutions is the formation of small groups or communities. These youth groups can be organized in parishes, neighborhoods, schools, universities or other places where youth meet. Groups are smaller units within the wider church organization. In small groups, young people can have a more personal experience of church.

b. Influence of Peer Group. Youth groups build on an important phenomenon of youth culture: the pressure of the peer group. The need to accept the life style of companions is an important factor in the formation of values. While many young people get satisfaction and status from conflict with adults, this is not so with regard to the peer group. Conflict with the peer group is avoided at all costs. Rejection by other young people is a traumatic experience for the young person.

Sometimes the peer group is formal, as is the case with church groups. Other times the group is informal. It may be a group of friends, a group that goes out together, a group that chats, supporters of a football team, or a street gang. Every large city has its places where, in practice, adults are excluded. The advantage of youth groups, within youth ministry is that they can channel the energy of the peer group in a positive way—and so make growth and integration possible.

Adolescence gives birth to a strong desire to be independent and be free from family and other symbols of authority. It is a period in which adolescents seek to establish their own identity by contesting the values of adults, family and infancy. During this period the peer group exercises significant influence, sometimes more than the family. When a young person has a problem, the first person he or she talks to is often not the father, or the mother, or the teacher, or the priest, but another young person. Youth groups aim at channeling peer pressure in a positive way toward growth and integration.

Reintegration into the family and the acceptance of values—previously rejected but now assimilated from personal conviction—is a sign that the passage to adult life is taking place. Youth groups can play an important role in facilitating a healthy transition.

c. Difficulties with Youth Groups. Youth groups are numerous in Latin America. In Brazil, for example, there are more than forty thousand groups attached to youth ministry. The majority are in parishes, although some are also in schools. Youth groups are less numerous in European and American dioceses. Unfortunately, most groups depend on a spontaneous process where there is little reflection or training in the necessary skills to make them work. Forming and accompanying groups is a great opportunity for a youth minister to help young people grow in their faith. Positive results will depend on our willingness to invest more time in this important area of youth ministry.

Groups can be formed through personal contact, courses, encounters, retreats, etc. The formation of youth groups was easier in the 1970s and 1980s. Today this task is more difficult because of more individualistic tendencies fostered by consumer society. Youth rarely come spontaneously to church-sponsored events. Many people are vying for their time and attention. Youth ministry has to compete with many other attractive options. A ministry-of-waiting must now be replaced by a ministry-of-outreach to young people. Today, the youth have more options for both leisure activities and serious commitment. Perseverance in the youth group is also more difficult than in the past. Boring, superficial and confused groups have little chance of surviving today.

Faced with the difficulty of forming and maintaining groups, some pastoral agents have concluded that the age for youth groups has passed. At the same time they are unable to present an alternative proposal—except that of remaining at the level of offering services to individual youth—with the limitations we have examined. This can be an easy way out for those who are not prepared for the "long haul" and are unwilling to make the option for a more professional approach to group work. Without investment of human and material resources we cannot expect encouraging results.

Some argue that investing in a parish youth group will lead to the abandonment of the other ninety-nine percent of the young people in the parish. That depends on your model of youth group. We are proposing here a model of youth group that avoids closing in on itself—that reaches out to other youth. Our model is the group of twelve initiated by Jesus.

Evangelization through groups is not a new methodology. Jesus invested much of his time in forming a group of twelve. After Pentecost it was this small group that continued his message. The members became the leaders of a new religious movement that was to sweep the world.

We make a distinction here between youth groups and youth clubs. Parish youth clubs are usually involved in organizing sporting events and dances for young people. The motivation behind such promotions often springs from a negative philosophy of keeping-youth-out-of-harm, rather than a positive goal of channeling their energies into transforming their environment. A faith dimension is usually absent and promotions differ little from government agencies that seek to keep kids off the streets.

Youth groups see sporting and recreational activities as peripheral. They prefer to put the stress on reflection and action. The aim is to channel the energy of youth into the renewal of church and society. Sporting and recreational activities are not excluded, but are integrated into a wider plan of formation and action. They are not center-stage.

d. Three Processes: Youth ministry must work on three fronts at the same time: Recruitment, Initiation, Commitment.

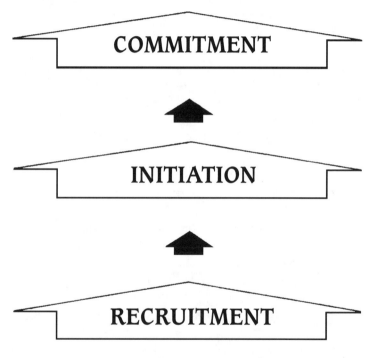

i) Recruitment Process. Recruiting involves inviting young people to form youth groups. It involves doing what Jesus did when he went out, selected people for his group of twelve and said to them: "Come, follow me." These groups are the basis of youth ministry. We need a strategy to form these groups, since young people rarely come spontaneously.

The formation of these groups is a question of life or death for serious youth ministry.

But first let us look at the target population of the youth we plan to penetrate. We can divide youth into **three groups**:

1) committed youth within the church
2) youth linked to the church through a sociological or cultural faith (faith without personal option and that depends on family pressure)
3) youth who are indifferent to the church (the unchurched)

Strategy Based on Three Levels of Youth Groupings

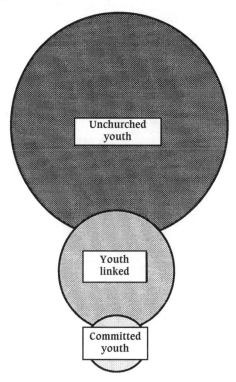

1) **Committed youth** are a small group. In general I believe it is not more than five percent of all baptized youth—perhaps one percent in some places. Each diocese can calculate its own percentage. This is the most important group. Through these young people, it is possible to build a bridge to the masses. With training and good methodology these can become the leaven to win over and mobilize the others.

2) **Young people linked to the church** are the ones that frequently go to mass, are confirmed, etc. but do not take on any commitment. Their contact with the church is motivated, in part, by family pressure, although there can at times be a personal option. Young people from this group usually come from practicing families. These youth can be very volatile. The link with the church is tenuous, since family pressure is effective, in general, only during adolescence. Later it no longer works and many abandon church practice. The group can constitute between five to thirty percent of Catholic youth, depending on the country and the region. Many in this group are favorably predisposed to cross the bridge into the committed group. Much, however, depends on the charisma of youth ministers and the methodology used.

3) **The indifferent youth (the unchurched)** are often the largest group. This group can be anything from fifty to ninety percent of Catholic youth depending again on the country and region. This is the group that is most influenced by the pluralism, individualism, and secularism of modern culture. The majority were baptized. Many have never spoken to the priest in their parish. Neither is the church a point of reference for their lives. Here is perhaps the greatest challenge for youth ministry. How do we get through to this group? In many places pastoral agents only work with the first two groups—the converted—and ignore the missionary challenge to go out to the remaining ninety percent of youth.

In some ways we seem to have gone back in this area. In the past the church had often more dynamic outreach programs to these youth. Specialized Catholic Action in the 1960s worked with young people in the different social milieus outside the parish. Youth encounters of the 1970s brought in many young people who had little contact with the church through a system of inscription forms and personal invitations for weekend encounters.

Strategies for Recruitment. The process of recruiting needs to consider the distance or approximation to the church of the youth being convoked.

There are two places where we can form new groups: in the parish community or in the social milieu outside (school, university, neighborhood, workplace). Most groups are formed in parishes. The following are some suggestions for forming new groups:

a) Personal and Systematic Contact. Personal contact is the most common method: one young person invites another to a retreat, encounter, meeting, or activity. The invitation of a young person to another young person is usually more powerful than that of an adult.

But personal contact is not just a hurried invitation made in a few minutes. Neither can it depend on general invitations read out at the end of Sunday mass. As a method it needs to be better structured. Personal contact is a process with its own stages that can take a few days or many months. The first step is to locate the young person to be invited—in the community, in the neighborhood, in the school, in the university, in the place of work or leisure. Sometimes youth who exercise influence over other youth or have potential for leadership are targeted.

In the group or coordination meeting, names of people to be invited are discussed; strategies are planned. In subsequent meetings there should be a follow-up on decisions taken. Without accountability, there is no seriousness and contacts are not valued.

A member of the Young Christian Students movement (YCS) told his story: "In class a student called Mark always remained withdrawn from the rest. Others treated him as odd and rarely talked to him. My group suggested I approach him. I discovered that the guy was only interested in one thing: stamp collecting. I bought a book on stamp collecting to be able to talk to him. I visited his home and we started going out together. When I had gained his confidence, I told him of the YCS, of my participation in the movement, of the importance of team work and the changes that a faith option had brought to my life. I invited him to participate in some events organized by the movement. He was impressed by the motivation and dedication of the other young people and their personal interest in him. His enthusiasm grew. Then the group invited him to help in the organization of a music festival. Mark became more involved and eventually asked to be accepted into the group. Later he became an important leader."

Sometimes people ask: "Should we invite beginners into a mature group or should we start a new one?" The above example illustrates a strategy for bringing a person into an already established group. It worked because Mark received special preparation. In general, if members of the group have had a lot of experience together, new people may feel displaced. It may be difficult to jump on a moving train—especially if it's going at a certain speed. Also more committed members may become frustrated if they are obliged to go back to previous stages to accommodate newcomers. There is a natural urge to continue a growth process. In most cases it's best to direct new candidates to new groups. There is, however, no strict norm. Each case has to be judged on its own merits.

A date has to be scheduled for the first meeting of a new group and time given to invite a sufficient number of people. The young person is often afraid to come alone to the first meeting and meet strange people. Leaders need to discuss means of surmounting this problem. A friend, for example, may volunteer to bring him to the meeting.

Neither should youth ministry be limited to one group in a parish. More groups can mean the emergence of more leaders and a richer exchange of experience. Working with just one group can signify "putting all the eggs in the one basket." When the basket falls, when a group fails, we lose everything.

b) Preparation for Confirmation. In most dioceses thousands of adolescents are confirmed each year. The reasons are varied. Many adolescents are motivated by pressure from parents. Others seek confirmation because of faith conviction. The length of preparatory courses can vary. The principal challenge is continuity afterward. One young person joked: "Theology teaches that confirmation is the sacrament of commitment, of Christian maturity. In my parish, however, it is the opposite. We have defined confirmation as a solemn ceremony, with the presence of the bishop, of graduation out of the church." After graduating with their "diploma of confirmation" many adolescents leave the church.

The "fall-out" is caused by the faulty methodology during the preparation period and the lack of concrete proposals for continuity. Confirmation programs based only on talks "turn young people off." Talks need to be complemented by creative dynamics that provoke active participation and interest. The secret of continuity is the organization of fixed groups during the time of preparation. The methodology and dynamics used should work toward this goal. A weekend retreat or encounter can bond young people together. Links of affection created during the course favor continuity. After confirmation young people frequently want to continue together because of the friendship created. They already form a group and so do not have to face the difficult step of approaching a new and strange group. Thus, youth ministry can be a natural continuity for these groups.

This type of proposal for continuity is more efficient than general appeals to become involved in "some activity in the parish" after confirmation. When the preparation for confirmation is well organized the parish can have a new experience of assisting in the birth of one, two, or three new youth groups each year.

c) Youth Encounters. Youth Encounters can be another powerful way of forming new groups. Many youth are unwilling to take on the more permanent commitment involved in belonging to a youth group, but will accept an invitation for a weekend Youth Encounter or Retreat. They are excited about getting to know new people and making new friends. There is a certain adventure in leaving home and staying with other companions in a different place. The encounter, however, must be well put together. Music, joy, and a welcoming environment are important. Talks and dynamics should challenge participants to look for something more in life. In their talks, youth leaders give personal examples of how they have faced the challenge of living the gospel message in their daily lives. Example is stronger than ideas. Ideas convince; example overwhelms.

During the encounter, discussion groups can be formed with a view to continuity. There is an advantage to having fixed groups during the entire encounter. Factors that help integration of members need be considered: people with similar interests, for example, are put in the same group. In each group a young person with experience of youth ministry methodology is put in charge so that he or she can continue as leader after the encounter. This move avoids a situation in which an experienced leader has to be introduced later as a stranger.

At the end of the encounter an invitation is made: "You have had an enjoyable experience together as a group, you have made many friendships, your vision of the faith and the world has been broadened. Why not continue meeting as a youth group?" In general, participants want to continue, motivated principally by bonds of friendship. Before separating, the group schedules its first meeting. Care must be taken to work out a timetable that fits into the busy schedule of most adolescents.

There are different types of Youth Encounters or courses. The preparation of the encounter needs to consider the group being targeted. If the young people have little participation in church life, the encounter will be lighter. When young people remain overnight in the place of the encounter, cohesion is built. Cost factors, however, may rule out this option. In such cases alternative solutions can be sought.

The difficulty with Youth Encounters as a tool for forming new groups is the time, energy, and number of people necessary to prepare the event. A coordination team that dedicates itself to this work soon finds there is no time for the other activities of youth ministry. This difficulty is being overcome in some places by training specialized teams exclusively for this work. Such teams are often made up of young married couples who have previously worked with youth.

ii) Initiation Process. The recruitment process can be the easiest step. An even greater challenge is what to do with a group after the first meeting. New challenges immediately present themselves. How do we continue maintaining a high level of motivation and participation in meetings? How do we launch a **process** that leads to conversion and concrete commitment? During the initiation process it's necessary to have a clear vision of **goals** (short, medium and long term), the **methodology** to be used and the **stages** to be reached. We describe these stages in more detail later.

iii) Commitment Process. Youth ministry needs to work on three fronts at the same time: **recruitment, initiation and commitment**. The committed youth are those who have a clear vision, who are prepared to embrace a cause, who have "sticking-power" when it comes to concrete projects, and who do not give up when obstacles appear. They are the leaders who decide the tone and quality of youth ministry.

Some youth take on internal commitment within the church, while others give priority to social commitment outside. The committed youth—especially those involved with social questions—need special guidance to deal with new and more advanced issues that spring from their involvement. There is now need for a theological, social, and psychological framework to support youth leaders who are becoming involved in public life issues. The lack of this specialized follow-up can mean a rupture in the process of evangelization and the impression that the gospel can be meaningful only for naive beginners. This difficulty has not yet been satisfactorily resolved within youth ministry.

3. Need for a Central Organization

A further level of development of youth ministry is related to the need for organization that will bring people together on a permanent basis. Isolation leads to impoverishment of ideas and experiences. Contact is necessary. In the scientific world, progress has come about through the exchange of ideas and experiences. Something similar happens in youth ministry. Isolation leads to dispersion of energy and lack of clear goals that challenge young people to grow and commit themselves. The organization of an organic youth ministry is therefore a very natural step. Organization leads to the formation of a network of youth groups and youth services. Through the network's communication lines there is a continuous flow of ideas and information. Collective action is now possible. The National Federation for Catholic Youth Ministry, founded in 1982 in the United States, is an example of a national umbrella organization that can perhaps function as a forum for the development of a more committed youth ministry on the lines we describe here. However the organization is still searching for more effective strategies for:

· involving young people on the level of decision making;
· passing from a model that is service oriented to one that is process oriented;
· improving internal democratic procedures that guarantee continuous formation and renewal of leadership.

Organization is therefore an essential step in building up youth ministry. Coordination committees are formed on different levels: parish, diocesan, regional and national. These commissions make possible the exchange of ideas and experiences in meetings, retreats, assemblies, encounters, courses, and musical festivals. Effective organization and structures are a guarantee of continuity. When talented youth ministers leave for other assignments everything does not collapse.

But the effort to organize involves doing ministry **for** youth, rather than doing ministry **with** youth. The temptation of bureacracy is a trap to be avoided. In some European countries that have a large budget for youth ministry I have found a negative reaction to organization because of a practice of organizing from the top down. With money and many salaried youth workers, youth ministry had been organized on the lines of a business firm.

The leaders were discovering that this type of organization does not work in a pastoral situation. The effective youth minister will want to avoid bureacracy by keeping in contact with active members on a local level. Organization should grow to meet felt needs—not the needs of beurocrats at the top of an organizational pyramid. Participation on all levels is important. People on a grass roots level must have a say in decisions taken by coordination committees. Organization needs to support a process in which theory and praxis (action that is reflected and evaluated) are being continually confronted and interrelated. But more about that later.

4. Importance of a Theory or Philosophy of Youth Ministry

Advance is possible only with a theory or philosophy of youth ministry. This fourth step is, perhaps, the most difficult. It's not sufficient to build an organization that facilitates the continuous flow, back-and-forth, of ideas and experiences. Youth leaders also need to be clear on two things: **where** they are going (vision) and **how** they are going to reach that vision (methodology). This means a theory or philosophy of youth ministry that is attuned to the aspirations of youth today. Such a theory must give meaning to young people's experiences, help them to understand complex realities and encourage them to become committed Christians. A theory helps leaders to understand a wide range of behavior and how to be more effective in working with young people. Without a theory or philosophy of youth ministry there is no clear direction. Youth leaders do a lot of pious splashing, but without making any headway. An integrated part of this theory involves growth through stages.

5. Stages of Faith Development
(Community and Social Model)

An important advance in this model was the discovery of different stages in faith. There is a progressive growth in faith. This model seeks to build a bridge between the real situation (indifference of young people today to organized religion) and the ideal to be reached (young people committed to Jesus Christ and his message within a church community. It is now clear to many youth leaders that there are different levels and stages in this process that must be considered. The gospel of Mark, the most primitive of the four gospels, shows a progression in the revelation of Jesus to his apostles. Faith development follows a gradual process that respects the law of nature itself. We need to learn the ABCs before we can write in English. The acquisition of all skills follows the same rules of nature. No skill can be acquired at once. It is the result of much repetition, effort, guidance, and challenge. There is no way of arriving at the top of the stairs except by taking each step at a time. The evangelization of youth must start on the ground floor with concrete life situations. Experienced youth workers know that the process is slow.

The belief that human growth involves passing through different stages is supported by the research of universally known theorists: **Jean Piaget** studied the evolution of human thinking; Erik Erikson calls attention to the way political, economic, and social structures, all exterior forces, mold a person's interior emotional life. In so doing, he seeks a union between psychoanalysis and the social sciences. **Lawrence Kohlberg** studied the evolution of moral thinking. **James Fowler** developed an important theory on stages of faith development. These pioneering works explain that the child is not simply a small adult, lacking only in physical growth. The human person passes through different stages of growth and development and this process has important repercussions for faith development. Faith needs to integrate all dimensions of the growth process, in a coherent and meaningful way, as it helps young people to overcome their crises and establish their identity. There should be no separation between body and soul, between prayer and action, between faith and social involvement. We were created by God as a unity. At times we may separate things intellectually to understand them better, but in the concrete person everything is interlinked.

Already in 1980 the U.S. youth ministry defined a developmental model that rested on five principles. The maturing of faith is a **gradual process** that depends on God's grace and also the interaction and environment we create; there are **distinctive stages**–this progressive growth is reflected in the **patterns of human development** and **faith development;** the culminating point is the **commitment** to some type of ministry.[5] Faith development, like all other types of growth, takes time. Just as we are not impatient with the slowness of physical growth, neither should we be discouraged with the slowness of growth in faith maturity.

In the United States, the publication of an important document, *A Vision of Youth Ministry,* in 1976, initiated a process of clarifying a theory of youth ministry. Other countries have followed. I believe we have much to learn from the experience and insights of one another. The building of a theory, however, is an ongoing process as new challenges continually demands adaptations and new focuses.

The following model of faith development through stages grew out of the Latin American experience of youth ministry. This model, which we will refer to as the **Community and Social Model** of faith development, has emerged as an answer to a felt need. Some youth leaders expected young people to commit themselves immediately. Efforts to go too fast and ignore stages of faith development led to failure and disillusionment. The need for some understanding of stage development became obvious.

This model has not fallen from the sky, nor been produced in the office of some inspired bureaucrat isolated from real experience with youth work. It is the result of the accumulated experience of more than fifteen years of youth ministry in Latin America and other countries. Many meetings, seminars, assemblies and study groups contributed to the clear focus we have today. Conclusions were continually confronted and tested with the concrete experience of young people. The exclamation of one young person reflects a common evaluation: "This theory is a photograph of my life. I have passed through all that." These conclusions were also studied in different Latin American youth encounters organized by the Youth Sector of the Latin American Episcopal Conference (CELAM). Over twenty-two countries were involved.[6]

The model also integrates the rich experience of specialized Catholic Action (Young Christian Workers, Young Christian Students, etc.). At one stage, for example, conversations with youth leaders in Spain played an important role in clarifying some of the stages we will describe presently. The methodology also has strong links with praxis theology and inductive methodology.

Stages were identified by examining the faith journey of the more committed youth. During a period of more than fifteen years these stages were observed; they were discussed and tested in many meetings and seminars. Finally there was agreement. It was now possible to define clear objectives and the different steps of the stairs necessary to encourage young people to continue climbing toward the goal of faith commitment. A principal cause of the superficiality of many youth groups could now be eliminated: the lack of clear goals and confusion about the road to be taken.

And so there was now a clear methodology for:

· socializing young people in a faith community;
· helping them to establish a personal relationship with Jesus Christ;
· preparing Christian leaders committed to the transformation of both church and society.

The following illustration summarizes the **stepping stones** we have described in the evolution of youth ministry:

Evolution of Youth Ministry

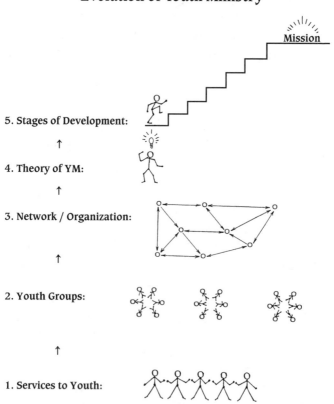

5. Stages of Development:

↑

4. Theory of YM:

↑

3. Network / Organization:

↑

2. Youth Groups:

↑

1. Services to Youth:

3

Stages of Faith Development (Community and Social Model)

We now have a clear pedagogy of stages to create favorable conditions for God's action in the young person's life. Faith is a gift of God; we cannot attain it with human effort alone. However, without creating favorable conditions, it is difficult to hear God's voice today. The following are the stages of the community and social model of faith development:

> 7. Discovery of Previous Stages
>   (Systematization of Whole Process)
> 6. Discovery of Commitment or Vocational
>   Option
> 5. Discovery of Structural Causes
>   (Social Analysis)
> 4. Discovery of Need for a Wider Organization
> 3. Discovery of the Social Problem
> 2. Discovery of the Community
> 1. Discovery of the Group

We can see the different stages as steps of stairs. The image of stairs describes a common reality in daily life. We can climb to the different floors of a building by taking one step at a time. But it is impossible to pass from the first step to the last in one stride. The most we can do is jump a few steps at a time. So we climb step by step. Faith development is similar. There are stages on the faith journey that must be known and respected.

These stages are described in the following pages. They show us the direction we need to take (short, medium and long term goals). They are a sort of road map for the journey that helps us locate where we are and where we are going in our group work. Without an understanding of the stages, one young person observed: "It is as if we were lost in the jungle, without a dog or a compass. We walk a lot; we use up a lot of energy. But we always seem to come back to the same place."

We are not presenting a radically "new" theory here. Rather we are helping people to perceive within a wider, dynamic process many things they are already doing. The stages outlined give a privileged place to individual growth through group or community experience. It is our belief nevertheless that people—even if they are not in groups—also pass through many of these stages by taking other paths. These stages are not a new proposal; we are rather helping young people to become aware of stages that are part of their faith journey. Many have already passed through these stages without being aware of having done so. Youth leaders need to understand these stages in order to help young people move forward to more advanced and demanding ones and avoid becoming imprisoned in their present stage.

Each stage starts with the word "discovery." Young people discover these stages on their faith journey. Youth ministry needs to create conditions for this discovery to take place. There are no short-cuts. The process of discovery cannot be substituted by a conference on the different stages. The theoretical knowledge in this chapter is important for the leaders, not for the beginners. Giving a talk on the stages will be meaningless to people who have not yet passed through them. A conference, however, can be important for leaders.

The following is a detailed description of each stage. A knowledge of this developmental sequence can be an important tool for youth leaders who are confused about the present and future direction of their groups.

1. Discovery of the Group

The young person needs a unit larger than the family, but not so large that he or she feels like a number in a crowd (as sometimes happens in a parish). "In the group the young person feels secure and valued as a person. He or she has the agreeable feeling of being among equals."[7] The group serves as a bridge between the family and a world that often appears threatening.

a. Space To Breathe a Different Atmosphere. Modern culture made it possible for the individual to emerge as a subject with rights. And this is positive. Independence and autonomy of the individual in relation to the wider group are emphasized. But this is only one side of the coin. The human person also needs community and social supports. "Many people live in situations in which they have to annul themselves as persons to continue living. The group constitutes a space where they can breathe a new freedom and be aware of their dignity," commented one youth minister. The importance of groups is further vindicated by modern psychology which uses group therapy to help people solve personal problems.

All young people, both poor and rich, feel the need to be valued and welcomed by others; they need to better their self-esteem. Young people are afraid of being ignored, of remaining alone. They discover the youth group as a solution for their isolation. In this new space they feel at home in the midst of other young people who have the same problems, the same language, the same values. There is an accepting environment for each to tell his or her history—a fundamental step in getting to know one another and creating a more profound level of communication and relationships. The young people want to be heard: they want to talk of their lives, their problems, their loves, their fears, their dreams. In the group other young people listen with attention. They feel valued— sometimes for the first time. There is an atmosphere of friendship, joy and enthusiasm. At this stage, personal relations are more important than doctrine. It is a stage in which the young people are concerned with themselves and their friends. Outside concerns are low on their list of priorities.

b. Resistance to Continuous Bombardment. Isolated, the young person has difficulty in resisting the continuous bombardment of misleading models and values that create an unfavorable environment for faith development. So we need to create new spaces where young people can breathe a less polluted air, where more idealistic values can be lived. This space, however, must not be understood as flight from the world. It is, rather, a space where one can refuel and put the pieces of one's inner life together—to return to the world as an agent of change.

Today, it is almost impossible to keep the flame of faith burning without the support of a group or community. "And so encourage one another and help one another, just as you are now doing" (1 Thes 5:11). A burning log glows only when it is in touch with other burning logs. On its own the flame dies. Thus, the youth group can be a privileged instrument for evangelization, for personal growth and social transformation.

c. The Group Has Yet To Be Born. The group is still not a group, nor is it a community. The group needs a warming-up period, in the same way as a car before starting. "It is obvious that the group is different from the human person, as it has its own laws based on the interrelation of a collective awareness. But it does pass through phases that are similar to those of individual growth."[8]

In the initial meetings, the group is at a "pre-natal" stage. It is an embryo that has not yet been born. At first there is a lot of inhibition and lack of initiative. The young people are cordial but are careful not to show too much confidence. People are afraid of making a mistake, of saying something stupid. The youth leader will not force the situation. One young girl arrived for the first time in a group and was immediately given a very difficult reading to do. She was very embarrassed. She never returned.

At this stage, there is still no group ideal. Each member has different expectations and values. Many are still evaluating if they will remain or not. Members drop out and newcomers arrive. The lack of stability and perseverance is a sign that the group is still not a group. The members are enthusiastic about practical activities and have little patience with study and deeper reflections. Parties, outings, games and dynamics can be important for eliminating barriers.

As the barriers fall, the joy and enthusiasm of participating together in meetings and promotions increase. It is, however, the emotion of the honeymoon that has not yet been tested in adverse situations. Initially the young people suggest big undertakings without taking into account their viability. As the group seeks to establish its identity it may create norms and rituals, give a name to the group, print special t-shirts to make public its new identity. As the members feel good together, there is a tendency for the group to close in on itself. At the beginning members are very dependent on the youth minister or leader. There is a paternalistic relationship that is necessary at the outset so that the group can move forward. Someone from the outside may coordinate the group: the youth minister or a more experienced youth leader. But the group needs to move gradually toward independence—to have its own life. At the beginning, it is as if the members are in a wagon and the leader is pulling it along. As the journey progresses, the leader encourages more and more people to get out of the wagon and pull it with him. And when this happens there is a great spirit of comradeship, of fun, of responsibility, and of mission. There is a parallel here with the human person. A person who remains dependent on parents is incapable of normal adult life.

The passage from "pre-natal" to "birth" depends on the climate created. It is difficult to decide a time for starting this passage. Each group is different. Some groups, however, are aborted, dying in the "pre-natal" stage. A competent youth minister can be very important during this phase.

Crises. As the honeymoon phase ends, tensions and misunderstandings arise. New qualities are now demanded of members, especially emotional maturity and capacity for self-analysis. Conflicts may lead to the formation of "cliques" around occasional leaders. The group passes through emotional swings: one moment it is "on a high" and another it is "on a low." Members are like a mound of loose stones. The crises are the cement needed to bind them together into a strong unity. When well directed, crises help members make the passage from the state of "being together" to the state of "youth group or youth community." However, a badly administered crisis can also lead to serious harm. When "there is a lack of appropriate pastoral support, these groups tend to dismantle when they face conflicts, especially internal conflicts. Sometimes the groups dismantle spiritually rather than physically, becoming just social clubs without a purposeful Christian spirit or mission."[9]

Perhaps this is the stage that requires greatest attention and greatest expertise on the part of the youth minister or leader. The latter "will help the members to look at the problems objectively, interpret them, separate the emotional from the objective facts and contribute with ideas for a deeper analysis. He or she is able to widen their vision and offer suggestions, refusing to give in to those who are content with little."[10]

The Group Takes Its First Steps. The transition starts. The group is born and tries out its first steps. "Little by little participants learn to respect each other's opinion and not to feel threatened by different viewpoints."[11] They learn to share, to work as a team and to forge common ideals together. Some young people stand out more, are more intelligent, have a wider vision and more initiative and are more sought after. They are the future leaders who need personal attention from the youth minister. There are others who are less gifted, but are valued for their human qualities, their responsibility, their common sense. The different personalities learn to pull well together and form a cohesive whole: the timid, the irritated, the introverted, the serious, the "clown," the distracted, the sensitive, the distrustful. The group acts as a stimulus for each to grow. One young person summed up her feelings about the group: "I feel good! People miss me; they like me in the group."

The mature group may have to deal with a very common and natural phenomenon during group development: members who manipulate, dominate or monopolize. The ability to handle the resulting tensions is a measure of group maturity. Members begin to own their group. Spontaneously they take on small tasks and responsibilities. Functions can be: vice-leader (an experienced leader will have already been chosen before the group started), secretary, treasurer, and time controller. New responsibilities develop talents placed at the service of others. Participation promotes emotional maturity. In an environment of freedom, young people make decisions and take on commitments that would be impossible in situations dominated by adults. New leaders emerge. Experience has shown that leadership is rarely formed outside the context of small groups.

To the extent that the individual establishes his or her own identity, the group advances toward group identity. The arrival point is the mature and cohesive group whose members are capable of self-criticism and of living in community and are open to the outside world.

d. How To Avoid an Early Death. The group is new. It can die easily. Care is taken that the young flickering flame is not allowed to die out. In the first meetings the young person is still evaluating the feasibility of remaining. Members start dropping out when meetings are tiring, badly coordinated and without preparation. On the other hand, members tend to persevere where there is good coordination and preparation.

Some youth leaders naively believe that **all** the youth have joined the group to deepen their faith or to build a better world. There is a danger here of using a deductive methodology that fails to start with the aspirations and needs of the young people themselves rather than their own felt needs. An inductive methodology will reveal that motivation is normally more mixed and subtle. In my courses, I have made surveys of the initial motivation of young people and gotten the following results: "I was tired of remaining at home and doing nothing, and I wanted to feel useful–I felt an emptiness taking control of my life–I wanted to date some girls–I went out of curiosity–I went because my two best friends participated (both have since left)–I wanted to change something and alone I couldn't–I was searching for sincere friendship and afterward I discovered Christ–My father always participated in church movements–I always participated in church activities–I wanted to know Christ better." Underneath the different motivations–even the most secular–is a searching for a religious experience that will give a deeper meaning to life. Nevertheless, the youth leader dare not ignore the real motivation of young people, for fear of building on foundations that are too feeble to sustain a serious youth ministry.

   e. Discovery of Christ as a Friend. And so, at this stage, the important emphases are: friendship, personal problems, the need to be valued, to feel useful, to discover Jesus Christ as a friend, the search for meaning in life. There is however an obstacle. One youth leader put it this way: "We frequently presuppose that young people today are turned on by Jesus Christ and the bible. On the contrary, many have a negative image of Christ and the bible–an image formed by years of boring religious education classes and an absence of religious formation in the family. Christ seems irrelevant to their lives. Youth who talk of Jesus are ridiculed as 'holy Joes.' So we cannot presuppose that young people are immediately attracted to Jesus Christ. An inductive methodology overcomes this obstacle by starting with young people's experience in order to prepare the ground. Only then, very often, can we plant the seeds of the word of God."

In a supportive environment young people are more open to the person and message of Jesus Christ and to respond to his call for commitment and conversion. Christ is now seen in a new light. For many adolescents the discovery of Jesus is made via the affections rather than the intellect. On the faith journey, the person of Christ is presented in a way that is attractive to young people. In a new environment they become receptive to certain gospel values such as acceptance of others, pardon, and solidarity. The gospel is read, discussed and related to their lives. It is no longer a series of boring texts and stories they have heard over and over again in religious education class. In discussion groups they relate different texts to their lives. The bible comes to life as it is explained and made relevant to what is happening around them. This is the Emmaus model that inspires adult youth ministers and youth leaders to reflect together on significant facts in their daily lives, in the light of Christian faith.

In this first stage, the group tends to function somewhat as a psychological clinic. The pedagogy of stages, however, pushes back the tendency to close in on itself in a "navel gazing" exercise. The next stage challenges the group to broaden its horizons.

2. Discovery of the Community

This stage explores an experiential and theological understanding of the church. We need to cultivate a sense of belonging-to-the-church in somewhat the same way as we develop emotional bonds of belonging to our families. It is part of our identity as Christians.

The young person made the first step by joining a group. In the group he learned to relate to others and to cultivate certain essential values for team work. The gospel and the person of Jesus Christ are understood and accepted in a new way. In an atmosphere of affection, faith is perceived as something that helps to form a frame of reference for the new identity that is being established. Faith is perceived as giving a deeper meaning to life.

Now young people take another step by bursting the restricted circle of the group and opening themselves to the wider reality of the parish community. Here the parish is the first reference for most youth. It's not the only place where young people can have an experience of a wider church community. But it continues being important as there are usually no other similar structures to receive young people. Nevertheless in the case of groups within a school environment, the experience of a school community can be an important step that facilitates entrance into the wider parish community.

Young people change a negative vision of church through contact with a meaningful religious experience rather than through the study of the theology of church. This does not mean that study is not an important part of young people's religious formation. Study however is frequently not an effective starting point. When young people participate in a meaningful church community an attractive vision of church becomes alive to them. To the extent that the young people participate in the life of the community, in parish celebrations, in recreational activities, and in courses, they make an important theological discovery: the church is a community of persons. The church is not just the priest nor the bishop. "We are the church" is the phrase that best sums up the awareness achieved at this stage. The church has now become meaningful and attractive.

a. Faith Presupposes a Community. The awareness of belonging-to-the-church is a fundamental element in Christian faith. Participation in the church community is the normal way of salvation. God wants to save us, not individually, isolated one from another, but as a people that live in community. The church is the group of persons who are convinced of the importance of following Jesus of Nazareth. "Christian faith is not possible except in and by the church. We can't meet the message of Jesus Christ except in the witness of other people who received the faith before us. God goes to meet humankind through human mediation; therefore the transmission of the faith presupposes a community as the necessary anterior context for the living and proclamation of faith in Christ."[12] The Bible presents us with an ideal model of the first community of Jerusalem that "was one in mind and heart" (Acts 4:32).

Theologically speaking, there is a fundamental equality between laity, sisters, brothers, priests and bishops. Through baptism all are co-responsible. This means a ministerial church where all its members exercise different ministries at the service of the common good. Authority is exercised as a service and not in the same way as the princes of this world to dominate others. St. Paul compares the togetherness in a community to the unity in the human body. The message of Jesus has visibility and credibility today because there are communities that meet and celebrate his presence and guide their lives according to his teachings. On the other hand, the church community does not exist for itself, but to be a sign of the God agape (love) and leaven of transformation in the world.

b. Negative Image of Church. However the reality that youth and adults too often meet is the "hierarchical-institutional" model of church. The absence of vibrant church communities creates a serious difficulty for developing a sense of belonging-to-the-church. The church, in many places, has little to say to young people. "An important discovery of the present phase of catechetical renewal is that the principal agent of catechesis is not the teacher or catechist, but the community of believers. The message embedded in the **way** of a community is more powerful than any textbook or blackboard message. And this is the problem that people who work with young people continually face in recent years: to find communities that personify the gospel, so that the young people can recognize the presence of Jesus."[13]

A major difficulty has been the attitude of many priests and adults of not welcoming young people. Some of our parishes have become bureaucratic and cold. They suffer from sclerosis. The people are an amorphous mass who come to "attend" mass on Sundays. There is no experience of community. The social dimension of the faith is ignored. A church that is not, before everything else, a community of faith that mirrors the light of God's love is off-putting to young people. Many youth opt out of celebrations they consider ritualistic and monotonous. The way they criticize indicates that many already feel themselves outside the church. Some, disillusioned with the religion offered by the church hierarchy, take refuge in a private faith; others become active in fundamentalist religious sects; others drift into secularized indifference.

On the other hand, there are also parishes, basic communities and dioceses that have engaged in a process of renewal. Sectors of the church have gained credibility for the institution by their prophetic stance on social problems and the development of warm, welcoming communities. These sectors exercise strong attraction for young people.

c. Invent Alternative Spaces. One of the solutions to the lack of vibrant parish communities is to help parishes to renew themselves. Organized youth ministry has been an important factor in nudging forward this renewal in many places. Where such renewal of the wider community is not possible, however, an alternative solution must be sought. New vital spaces for young people need to be created within the church institution. In a modern culture that rejects authoritarianism and imposition, the church can only gain credibility to the extent it creates these spaces where young people can participate and make decisions. These must be spaces where gospel values can become visible and that serve as a reference point for youth. They are spaces where young people can have an experience of church as community and force of transformation in an unjust society. Such a space is, especially, although not exclusively, the youth group, linked to a network of other groups under the umbrella of youth ministry. The diocesan youth ministry can be an important point of support and formation where parishes are not welcoming to young people. One Irish youth minister put it this way: "Through the diocesan youth ministry we get fishing rights in all parishes. We are able to get into places that would be otherwise closed to us and organize young people and link them to a wider diocesan network where they are motivated by the enthusiasm and commitment of their peers."

We are not talking here about creating a parallel church, but of making the group, the encounters and retreats a meaningful experience of church. For many young people this may be the only possible mediation, due to their special circumstances. Then the group is the sacrament, the visible sign that leads the young person to a salvific encounter with God and to take personal decisions that can change life's direction. It is not the only sacrament of God's presence; in certain circumstances however it can be a decisive one.

The emphasis on alternative vital spaces for young people must not be seen as the removal of pressure on the institutional church to change. The contrary, in fact, is frequently the case. Where possible, youth energy can be channeled toward church renewal.

Many groups also become involved with the great questions of our time: poverty, marginalization of women, racial discrimination, the destruction of nature, and urban violence. Their involvement is a sign of hope for the poor and renews the church as the sign of God's reign in society.

Thus the group that meets in the name of the Lord evangelizes other young people who seek reasons for living. At the same time, the strength of the group as mediation is greater when it is part of a wider dynamic ministry, on diocesan and national levels. The wider organization offers a substitute for the anonymity and mediocrity of some of our parishes.

d. Utopian Image of Community. But many young people become frustrated because their expectations for church community are too high. Youth leaders need to lower expectations, to be more realistic. When the utopian image of community is confused with real life, young people end up discouraged. The utopian image is the ideal of community presented by Jesus in the gospels. We are challenged to attain it. An ideal however is like the stars; they are far away; they show direction. The stars in ancient times helped guide navigators in the right course. And just as we can never extend a hand and touch a star, neither can we achieve an ideal situation in this life. We can never build a perfect community. The ideal of the perfect community, however, is important to motivate a continuous growth process. But we need to avoid the "tyranny of the ideal" by being realistic and recognizing our limited human condition.

There is no such thing as a perfect community without conflict and pain. Community involves the collision of people with different personalities, ideas and behavior patterns. Community is like the fire that refines the gold. "In community God wants us to learn something about ourselves, our limits, the need we have for others. In this process there is the pain of not being able to impose our way, but the promise of finding **the way**....But the people who manage to survive the failure of their dream and the pruning of their egos will find strong support in community and a richer reality than fantasy can ever offer. Because in community one learns that the individual is not the prefabricated measure of reality; that we can begin to know the plenitude of truth only through multiple visions."[14] A community teaches us that when we look to one another we find God. We need many listeners to learn and understand the richness of revelation. Working and living together we learn that the only trustworthy power is situated beyond human structures. In the last analysis it is faith in God's presence that makes community possible. "For where two or three come together in my name, I am there with them" (Mt 18:20).

The dimension of community is an important contribution of the church to modern culture. We need two anchors to navigate in the turbulent waters of modern life: on the one side is the autonomy, initiative and courage of the individual; on the other side is the need we have for a supportive community. Unfortunately, for many people the anchor of community has been wrenched away and individualism has become the only norm to avoid shipwreck on the treacherous rocks of isolation. Many today are adrift without human warmth or community support. Both anchors are important. People need the courage to stand alone, but also the capacity to stand together.

e. Relationship with the Hierarchy. Therefore we need to value the youth group as mediation and experience of church—in some circumstances the only one possible. Simultaneously, we must be aware of its limitations. Somehow the group has to be linked with the rest of the church, especially with the local community. Westerhoff points out that this wider community needs to be small enough so that each one can be recognized as a member, be intergenerational because every community needs memory and vision. If there are only young people, memory is very limited and there is little diversity. The wider community is a richer experience, not limited to one age group. In bridging this gap the adult youth minister is a key player.

In the wider parish community it is easier to cultivate a eucharist spirituality. It is also a guarantee of continuity as groups are a passing phenomenon while community is permanent. When the parish is divided into small basic communities, relationships can be more profound. Participation in a wider diocesan ministry also prevents groups from turning in on themselves and forming "parallel churches" that eventually become isolated and superficial.

On the other hand groups bring a richness to the church's life. Those involved with social issues, for example, bring a new awareness and understanding to the wider church; in this way the process of evangelization can "take root with vigor" (see Puebla Document 795).

So the young person develops a sense of belonging-to-the-church by living in a faith community. But we cannot remain only on the level of experience. A more intellectual foundation is necessary if we are to have a solid basis for this new way of life. At this stage the study of models of church[15] becomes important. It is a relief for the young person to discover that the authoritarian and clerical model that he or she rejects is not the only model. There are others: more authentic, more biblical, more liberating, and relevant to social reality. Young people are now motivated to study the theological basis for a more authentic model and be part of an ever increasing swell of people who are building a new church.

Young people need to avoid the temptation of rupture with the hierarchical church. At the same time, adult youth ministers need to be aware that some adolescents feel the need for a temporary separation from the church just as they do from their families. It is not necessarily a definite life stance. It can be a painful beginning of faith. Groups go through different phases here. At first there is often a generalized criticism of priests. Meetings can give the impression that all difficulties are reduced to this single problem. The more mature leaders are more realistic. Where it is possible to win over uncooperative pastors, young people have effective strategies for doing so. At the same time, they are realistic. They recognize the difficulty of changing the mentality especially of some priests who have little capacity to change. The more mature youth leaders realize that the energy consumed in useless conflicts can be channeled to removing other obstacles that are blocking the advance of youth ministry. It is not good strategy to concentrate on an insurmountable obstacle while other more positive growth avenues go unattended. One needs to choose one's battles. In a diocesan evaluation assembly one youth leader gave vent to his frustration: "We have many beginners here who are still at a phase of wasting all their ammunition on priest-bashing while the more experienced leaders want to discuss other problems whose solutions depend on us."

3. Discovery of the Social Problem

Young persons enter the group. Their vision widens to include different aspects of life in community: team work, self-knowledge, capacity to relate to others, personal relationship to Christ. Breaking through the closed circle of the group of friends, they discover the richness of a wider church community. They become enthusiastic with the discovery of a community model of church that is attuned to their own ideas. But now the horizon of the local church community has become too limiting. This circle is now ruptured and young people are thrown into a new world: the drama of surrounding society.

a. Compassion and Solidarity. Previously young people had a vague awareness of the problems of surrounding society. They could see people asking for alms in the streets, pass in front of a slum area, see on television the drama of starving families in some impoverished country. But the scenes never seemed to register. The problems were distant. The young people were turned in exclusively on themselves and their immediate friends. Politics was considered synonymous with corruption and demagogy. The lives of many were taken up with futilities. The media were also an important ally in helping with the flight from the brutality of the real world to a land of dreams and fantasy.

There is now a major change in young people's outlook. The programs of the group and the wider youth ministry have helped them to look more closely at what is happening outside the group. Social problems are no longer seen as distant and abstract issues. Young people now feel responsible for the wider human family. They feel the need to make a difference. There is an urge to do something to help, to alleviate human suffering. The natural idealism of youth had been made dormant by a materialistic/consumer society. But now the sentiments of compassion and solidarity are being tapped. Youth ministry in some dioceses gives special emphasis to this phase. The archdiocese of Philadelphia, for example, has a highly organized "Community Service Corp." Many schools organize service programs so that students can have personal contact with marginalized sectors of the population. Services can take many forms: helping with soup kitchens, visits to prisons and homeless shelters, work in hospitals, writing letters to prisoners, adopting a poor mother about to have a baby. Some schools have similar service programs based on the philosophy that it is good for young people to have contact with people who are less fortunate than themselves. Contact with disadvantaged people helps young people to have another perspective on social problems. They learn that it is good for neighbor to help neighbor. The world we build does not have to be one in which dog-eats-dog.

During the first stage, personal problems were the center of most discussions. Now young people perceive their problems as tiny in comparison with the sea of suffering and pain around them. They are moved by the marginalization of large sectors of the population. The gap is now being bridged in regard to what the Vatican Council calls the greatest error of modern times: the divorce between faith and life.

Who Is My Neighbor? The central message of Jesus is now being discovered in meetings, talks, and courses. The bible comes to life. It is no longer a dull textbook that is studied in school for exams. The message of the good Samaritan, of the last judgment, of the new commandment is very clear. To be a Christian is not a question of studying religion, of **knowing** the right answers. Christianity is more doing than knowing. Being a Christian involves more than sitting at meetings. It's necessary also to move toward action. Young people are now aware that "faith without action is dead" (Jn 2:20). They want to help; they want to do something to lessen other people's suffering. They want to be on the side of the "underdog." And so the gospel option for the poor becomes their option also.

Suggestions are made for campaigns to help the poor, to visit orphanages, hospitals and prisons, to organize presents for underprivileged families at Christmas. At this stage, contact with human suffering becomes an important part of youth formation. Contact reveals the gravity of social problems. The members of one youth group visited the families of their neighborhood to do a parish census. They discovered families living in conditions of extreme poverty. The young people were appalled. They were living in the area but had been unaware of the problem. The shell that had isolated them from reality had come apart. One girl remarked: "It was only when I started working with teenage mothers that I realized how encapsuled I was from the real world."

The themes of group meetings and courses now undergo a significant change. More vital themes are discussed: the cost of living, violence, racism, hunger in the world, child abuse, corruption. Christ is seen as identifying himself with the poor and with the marginalized. The feeling of compassion leads to action in favor of the underprivileged. At this stage, young people develop an attitude of service to others, an attitude that undermines the individualistic ideology of modern culture.

b. Naive Vision. In this third stage, young people's vision of the social problem is still descriptive and naive, and actions aim at eliminating effects rather than causes. Problems are considered in isolation. There is no global or structural vision of society. Neither is there a critical awareness. One young person, in an inner city area, relates her experience: "We organized a campaign to help the poor of our neighborhood. The poor were the others. It was only later we realized that we too were disadvantaged and needed to unite to create awareness and bring about change."

More advanced and critical youth leaders sometimes poke fun at the young people who are at this stage. They have difficulty in accepting their naive analyses. They fail to perceive the formative value of contact with human suffering and the development of an attitude of service. Young people will advance to a further stage to the extent they are encouraged and helped to reflect critically on their experiences.

c. Vocational Awakening. The sports and "pop" models, fabricated by consumer society, gradually lose their force of attraction. Jesus becomes the central life model. His life style and message challenge the young people to no longer talk of Christian love in the abstract. It is time now to act. Thus conversion as a response to Christ's call becomes more real.

Openness to others and willingness to serve them is the first step in the maturing process of the Christian vocation. Paul VI reminds us: "Vocation signifies the ability to listen to the voices of the innocent, of those who suffer, of those who have no peace, who lack the basic needs, who have no guidance or love." We can situate here an important point of contact between youth ministry and vocational ministry.

4. Discovery of a Wider Organization

This stage occurs when the young people move beyond their group and community and maintain contact with the **wider youth organization.** They discover "youth ministry." Their group is no longer isolated. Many other groups, with the same ideals, are going in the same direction. Their influence and strength increase to the extent they are part of a network of youth groups. They now have a powerful voice within the church. Youth power has been harnessed for transformation.

Participation in some event organized by youth ministry can be the rite of passage to this stage. Again the primacy of experience over theory. A young person may be elected as a representative of the group or diocesan coordination team, or may participate in a course, a retreat, an encounter, a youth rally. Previously youth ministry was something abstract, distant. Now that young person knows people who are leading the organization, is excited with the new friendships, and is strongly affected by the conviction of the more committed youth.

a. Isolation Impoverishes. The new way for forming people today is by getting them to coordinate their own activities and work together. This is an important step for youth groups. Isolation impoverishes. An isolated person has little influence or possibilities for growth. Similarly isolated groups run out of alternatives for development and begin to repeat themselves. They are groups adrift, disconnected from the whole. Many good initiatives on the local level run out of fuel due to lack of more ample diocesan or even national structures where they can situate themselves.

Isolation is perhaps the factor that most militates against acquiring a critical awareness of reality. The difference between youth is immediately obvious in a coordination meeting or assembly of delegates. The young people who arrive for the first time are naive and lost. On the other hand, critical awareness advances rapidly where groups are interlinked through a coordinated network. Contact with other more committed youth and adults accelerates the learning process. There are many opportunities to exchange ideas with people of different experiences and perspectives. There is a continuous flow of new ideas and information—in courses, retreats, seminars, assemblies, and encounters. An awareness grows that "organized injustice" can only be overcome by "organized action."[16] Action can now be planned together. Together young people feel empowered to bring about change.

This model of youth organization is perhaps best developed in Latin America where there is an organizational structure that goes from the youth groups on a grass roots level to a continental coordination team. This involves a great number of youth, in a more complex organization. It also involves a pastoral plan elaborated with goals, content, methodology and programs. Such a pastoral organization makes possible contact with other groups and other young people in ever widening circles of influence through coordination meetings, assemblies, courses, retreats, congresses, festivals, rallies, news bulletins, newspapers, radio programs, walks, and recreational activities. The exchange of ideas and experiences continually gives birth to new horizons of growth.

A well-run youth ministry responds to young people's need for solidarity, participation and responsibility. Young people at this stage are more committed and are highly motivated to persevere. They are in youth ministry for the long haul.

Scaffolding. Organization makes it possible to accumulate pastoral experiences in a systematic way so that there are clear goals, methodology, group-spirit, and spirituality. Each new group does not have to invent everything again. They can build on the advance that has already been made. Experience has shown that without structured support, without more ample programming, it's impossible to develop the rich possibilities of serious youth work. Organization is the scaffolding for bringing young people together and building a youth ministry that can continually adapt itself to young people's needs. Also organizational structures such as election of leaders, coordination committees, participative planning and evaluation are a guarantee of internal democracy and continuity. Thus, when a charismatic leader leaves the organization, continuity is not threatened.

b. Empowering Young People. Organization should promote young people as protagonists—as actors. Research has shown that the most effective education is when teens talk to each other. The way youth ministry is organized should empower youth. When this is so, young people come to see youth ministry as belonging to themselves rather than to adults. Participating in decisions is a necessary step to empowerment. Young people need to be involved in coordination committees and evaluation and planning sessions. Decisions are based on the strongest arguments and conclusions arrived at through consensus or voting. In this way, young people have their own space within the institutional church. They drive a vehicle in which the steering wheel is in their own hands. I have been present in many evaluation and planning sessions where young people were involved in elaborating their annual pastoral plan. Some topics involve intense debate. Young people learn the skills of public speaking by standing up and presenting their ideas in an organized way. Before voting, they are obliged to follow closely the different positions to distinguish the best proposal. The act of raising hands to vote has a powerful effect on the formation of leaders, the creation of a group spirit, and the empowerment of young people. Youth ministry can have no greater duty than to prepare young people for leadership in today's society.

In many situations today, young people have the opposite experience. They are rarely invited to participate in decisions that affect directly their own lives, in the school, in the family, in work, in politics. One young person commented: "I have noticed that the young people take on serious commitment only when they feel they **own** youth ministry. In real life they are often not valued. Their ideas are dismissed. I participate because I like to; I feel I am always growing. Some church leaders, however, believe that young people should be passive receivers; they see them as so many empty containers to be filled with information."

Paternalism and authoritarianism are the cancer that undermines youth empowerment. Many religious and lay adults tend to make decisions alone, to do things without involving young people. Afterward they are disappointed because the youth are disinterested. They fail to understand an important psychological fact: the best way of motivating people to carry out anything is to involve them in the previous decision making process. In a diocesan annual assembly the priest youth minister made all the announcements, explained the different dynamics, coordinated everything. He remained center-stage all the time while the youth leaders were reduced to a role of office boys carrying out errands. This paternalist or authoritarian attitude (they are two sides of the same coin) is the mortal enemy of youth empowerment. Sometimes the argument of greater efficiency is used to justify this approach. Efficiency and speed in decision making are given priority and participation and growth are pushed aside. The cost of such an approach is high. For those who stay, it can result in the formation of Christian youth with the emotional age of children.

Empowerment means helping young people to throw aside the crutches and learn to walk on their own. However, not all sectors of the church feel at ease with young people who have their own ideas and personalities since consequences cannot always be foreseen. Control is more difficult. Empowering youth involves taking risks. But then again this is the only road to maturity.

c. Young People as Evangelizers. Young people are the first ones responsible for their own growth in faith. They have greater possibility of benefiting from a formation program when they themselves participate in its elaboration and execution. Young people evangelize other young people in meetings, courses, and assemblies by their example of faith and dedication, through their contributions to discussions, and by their commitment and action. There are no better evangelizers of young people than their own companions.[17] Here the influence of the peer group is especially important.

At this stage the vision of church is no longer restricted to the territorial limits of a parish. There is a growth in awareness of the universal church and a perception of a living, vibrant community, and of a faith incarnated in real life situations.

d. Organizational Skills. Where some groups are not linked to the wider youth organization a strategy needs to be devised to involve them. That is one side of the coin! The other side that needs to be considered is the health of the youth organization itself. An inefficient diocesan coordination can, in fact, be an obstacle to group participation. Sometimes members of the coordination committee are confused and have no leadership skills. Superficiality in youth organization becomes a certain road to failure. There is no point in bringing in representatives from groups if the coordination committee is insolvent. The success of this model of youth ministry, therefore, depends on the quality of its leadership.

But young people have a serious difficulty here. Due to their age, they have little experience of organizing. Many young people can find themselves in a leadership position without knowing how to coordinate a meeting, conduct a debate, distinguish between different proposals, help to arrive at concrete conclusions, prepare an agenda, follow up on decisions taken, involve others in a planning process, control a budget, and coordinate many things simultaneously without getting lost. In an organization, people and groups need to cooperate to build a common project. It is like the cogs of an engine. If all the cogs are spinning independently but are not making contact, the engine does not function. The gear lever must bring the cogs into contact so they can work together to propel the car forward. The coordination committee is the lever that makes it possible for the different groups to pull together in a common project. A faulty lever makes progress difficult. So the adult advisor and the more experienced youth need to create programs and conditions for young people to acquire these leadership skills.

There are, of course, other reasons why coordination committees fail. The youth group may, for example, send as its representative the member who has less capacity, the one who is not "serious about anything" or the one who is doing nothing. Such groups have not yet grasped the role of the coordination team as the "think-tank" and "helmsman" of youth ministry. Other groups may send a different representative each time, making continuity impossible. Putting beginners into leadership positions too early is another difficulty that can lead to burnout and opting-out. One young person had a rocket-like ascension. Within four months of entering a youth group he was elected leader of the group; later he was elected area representative; in the area he was elected onto a diocesan coordination committee; in the diocesan coordination committee he was elected to a national coordination committee. He got lost in a multitude of meetings where he lacked the skills for working on more difficult and wider levels of coordination.

There is also a cultural factor that can influence organization. The associative tendency is stronger during some periods more than others. In the 1970's this tendency was strong; today it is weak, thus making the organization of youth ministry more difficult.

5. Discovery of Structural Causes

Now young people have conditions for taking another step to expand the horizon of their world vision. Adolescents are at what Piaget calls a stage of formal operational thinking. They discover in themselves a new ability for logical and abstract thinking. This ability can be nurtured by creating a critical awareness of the world in which they live. Young Christians need to learn to approach problems without blinkers. Blinkers are for horses, to keep them from taking any direction other than that intended by their masters. This is, without doubt, the most critical stage, the most difficult, the most complex. For this reason we will delay longer in describing it.

We call this stage the "discovery of structural causes." A word first about structures. Structures are institutions and practices (economic, social, and political) created by people. "Being necessary in themselves, they often tend to become fixed and fossilized as mechanisms relatively independent of the human will, thereby paralyzing or distorting social development and causing injustice."[18] Although structures exercise powerful influence over us, we can change them.

a. Structures Are Invisible. Unjust and manipulating structures are more dangerous since they are invisible and distant. They are especially dangerous since most people are unaware of them. People can see the violence of a street kid who robs a bracelet from a wealthy person but are unaware of the institutional violence of an economic policy that lowers wages or increases unemployment—with the consequent break-up of family life.

Leaders of Germany's Protestant and Catholic churches put it this way: "Poverty is not a marginal problem of society. Poverty is not simply individual fate. Poverty is a structural problem, caused by the particular setup of the societal, economic and social order. Therefore, it is a co-responsiblity of the community to ensure an adequate living standard for its disadvantaged members. It should not be allowed to exclude or stigmatize people in need or suspect them of misusing public payments."[19]

Economic and political structures determine that billions of dollars are spent annually on sophisticated arms to kill. The same quantity of money would be sufficient to solve most social problems in the world today. Economic structures are today destroying unrenewable natural resources necessary for future generations.

Structures exercise enormous influence over people's behavior and quality of life. Few young people, for example, are aware that their pop idols are fabricated by marketing structures. So also the type of clothes they use, their attitudes to sex, to religion, to justice, to solidarity. Young people suffer massive campaigns to manipulate their needs. What is more serious, they are not aware of being manipulated. They fail to perceive that their choices, behavior and values are influenced, and, at times, determined, by decisions taken by a group of business people who meet in New York, London, Tokyo or some other economic center of the world. People who are responsible to nobody make decisions, in secret, that determine the quality of life of millions.

A major flaw in the development of youth ministry in many countries is the absence of this stage (discovery of structural causes). "Young people in our society are one of the most manipulated sectors of the population. They are oppressed because they don't have an active voice and therefore feel powerless; they are manipulated because they are unaware of structures and systems that control their lives. These structures and systems include the educational structures, economic structures, especially the structures of marketing and advertising, political structures, religious structures (especially organizational structures of parishes and dioceses). Awareness (of these structures) is linked with politicization....Naturally a politicized youth will want to have an active voice in the adaptation of structures that exercise influence over them, including schools. This is perhaps one of the reasons why teachers dedicate such little time to help young people understand the functioning of power."[20]

Many people who work with youth ignore not only the influence of economic and political structures, but even the more obvious structures of communication, such as films, magazines, and music. They can acquire an ability for critical thinking by starting with an analysis of the powerful modern means of manipulation that determine how many youth think and act. Young people acquire a capacity to distinguish between values and counter-values. They realize that a new society will mean reforming different structures: agrarian, political, habitation, health, and distribution of income. It will also mean setting people free from the chains of manipulation and passivity.

b. Cutting the Weed's Head. This is the stage of social analysis, of asking "why," of discovering deeper causes. Like the doctor we observe the symptoms to diagnose the cause of society's ailments. Social problems are like weeds. If we cut off the head, they will grow again. We need to dig deeper to find the roots—the root causes. Long term solutions are possible only insofar as we attack root causes. Many "good" people in the last century advocated the need to treat slaves well, but failed to see the need to question the structure of slavery itself. We are doing the same today with other social problems.

This is a very political stage—a stage that can be conflictive. Bishop Helder Camara observed once: "When I give food to the poor, I am called a saint. But when I ask why the poor have no food, I am called a subversive." This awareness unveils the liberating dimension of youth ministry. Reality can no longer be limited to the psychological and subjective! Religious commitment is now evaluated in terms of its contribution to the building of a new world. Action must be preceded by an analysis of causes to avoid attending to the fever while ignoring the infection—of giving an aspirin to cure an appendix.

Perhaps the word that best defines this stage is the

word CHANGE. Youth leaders need to work at changing the world because it is not as God would have it. Motivation for this change comes from awareness of three factors:

· today's social problems are grave;
· the rate of change depends on the degree of discontent;
· the efficacy of change depends on a knowledge of deeper structural causes.

c. Giving the Answer Too Early. More conscientized leaders are often tempted to precipitate the gradual discovery process by giving answers on the level of structural causes to questions that young people are not yet asking. In my early years as a youth minister I fell into this trap when I accompanied a youth group that had just begun to visit a slum area of a large city. The group was still at the third stage ("discovery of the social problem"). I gave the members a talk on the mechanisms of manipulation in society. The lack of interest and the incapacity of my listeners to assimilate a wider and more critical vision of society were soon apparent. The transition to a new stage of awareness required more than a simple talk. I had made an important breakthrough: the discovery of structural causes is a slow and complex process. The talk could have been at a later stage. Young people needed first to reflect, in the light of the gospel, on the experiences that came out of their visits—and then to draw their own conclusions. This type of continuous reflection on facts related to their visits would eventually create the desire for a more scientific theory to help understand the isolated facts within a coherent whole. A more scientific theory—necessary to identify structural causes—could only be presented when the young people were ready for it. More will be said later when we discuss the interaction method of theory/praxis.

However, as young people awaken to the gravity of social problems we have to avoid an atmosphere of paralyzing negativism. Youth leaders must swerve from the danger of becoming prophets of doom and gloom. One youth minister advises: "The question is how to form critical awareness without entering a counter-productive circle of bitterness and of lamentation."

d. Option for the Poor. This stage takes seriously the option for the poor in the social documents of the universal church and local bishops' conferences. The option for the poor is the thermometer for measuring the spiritual health of the church. The poor, as the sacrament of the presence of Jesus Christ, becomes an important part of youth spirituality. "I tell you, whenever you did this for one of the least important of these brothers of mine, you did it for me" (Mt 25:40). The American bishops remind us:

> Poverty is increasing in the United States, not decreasing. For a people who believe in "progress," this should be cause for alarm. These burdens fall most heavily on blacks, Hispanics, and Native Americans. Even more disturbing is the large increase in the number of women and children living in poverty. Today children are the largest single group among the poor. This tragic fact seriously threatens the nation's future. That so many people are poor in a nation as rich as ours is a social and moral scandal that we cannot ignore.[21]

In the bible God is not neutral. Both the New and the Old Testament present God as taking sides. Again and again he makes an option for the disadvantaged. The church has always made an option for the poor—promoting works of mercy, giving food to the hungry, visiting the sick. Throughout the ages it has built hospitals, schools and orphanages.

At the end of the 1960s, however, a new understanding of the option for the poor emerges. Young people linked with Specialized Catholic Action (worker youth, university and secondary students), especially in Latin America, are influential in bringing about this change. Traditional methods of solving social problems are seen to be largely ineffective. Handouts are ineffective in solving social problems. Social sciences can help with a more scientific understanding of cause and effect. It is now obvious that getting at the effects, the symptoms, of poverty is not sufficient. The causes have to be addressed and eliminated. The question needs to be asked: Who is producing so many poor people in a world that for the first time has the capital and technology to eliminate poverty? The problem is not the poverty but the "mechanisms that generate poverty" (Puebla Document 1160) and the lack of political will to eliminate social discrimination. It is a problem of greater production but also one of distribution of income. So the factory that manufactures poor people has to be deactivated if we are to build a better world.

In our present economic system this exploitation takes place mainly through the conflict between capital and labor. The quality of life of most people depends on their labor. Work is the key to most social problems, especially poverty. We live in a world in which capital (money) gives the orders and determines the rules of the game. Thus "the rich become richer at the cost of the poor who become increasingly poorer" (John Paul II at Puebla). This is especially true of third world countries, but in first world countries "money also talks."

Justice is the fruit of negotiation, but especially of social pressure. Capitalism is an economic system that distributes under pressure. It attends those who pressurize most. For this reason marginalized groups need to be empowered and promoted so they overcome their negative self-image and insist on their rights (see Puebla Documents 132-136). Two things are necessary to increase the bargaining power of workers in the conflict between capital and labor: awareness raising and organization.

e. The Perspective of the Impoverished. Many third world countries have a social pyramid somewhat like this:

SOCIAL PYRAMID

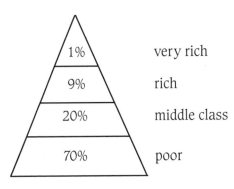

1%	very rich
9%	rich
20%	middle class
70%	poor

Income is also concentrated in first world countries, although to a lesser degree. These latter usually have a much larger middle class, which is the secret of their stability.

Every point of view is the view from the point where we are standing. Where we are standing in the pyramid shapes our point of view; it gives us the perspective from which we view reality. The perspective will determine the lenses we use, and these in turn determine our vision of the world around us. There are two types of lenses: those that look at the world from the top of the pyramid and those that look at it from the bottom. In each case the vision is different. Those at the top, in general, are satisfied with the situation and are against change. It benefits them financially and otherwise. Those at the bottom want to change the situation urgently as they are crushed by social, economic, and political structures over which they have no control. This is the perspective of "the tired, the poor, and the huddled masses," ancestors of many of today's middle and upper class Christians.

Today the notion of perspective is used to understand the point of view not only of the poor, but also of all oppressed groups in society. This is where the three great movements of our time come together: social oppression, racial oppression, and sexual oppression. A poor black American girl, for example, suffers all three types of oppression and will have a very different story to tell than the white American middle class girl. A black American boy, living in an inner city area, will have a different story to tell than a boy of European extraction living in a middle class area of the same city. We need to listen to both stories to understand what is going on in society. Understanding the perspective of others is always important, whether it be on the level of personal relations or whole sectors of society. But especially analyzing events from the perspective of the disadvantaged can change radically how we organize youth ministry. One young person commented: "We may discover that we have a hidden agenda. That what we say, write and organize is for middle class kids—with some sops for justice and peace to alleviate guilt feelings. We have unconsciously excluded disadvantaged youth from our youth organization."

But the present social organization has to be justified and presented as something that benefits everyone. This justification is possible through ideology. The strong emotional and unconscious elements in ideology explain why people can be supportive of unjust structures while believing they are defending the common good. While there are many different ideologies in society, the dominant ideology is the ideology of the dominant class. It is largely unconscious. This ideology uses lenses that look at the world from the top of the social pyramid. Poor people are seen as responsible for their poverty. In a situation of conflict the people without power are blamed. The victims are responsible for being victims. The situation is justified ideologically by such frequently repeated statements that the poor are poor "because they want to be," "because they don't work hard enough," "because they are lazy and want to live off welfare," "because they can't administer their money," "because they drink a lot" or "because they don't study."

The American form of capitalism, more so than the European, has tended to maintain a suspicious and punitive attitude to poor people. Their poverty is seen as personal failure rather than a problem of the economic system.

For those who use the lenses of the poor the perspective is different. It is true that some disadvantaged people are lazy. But what about deeper structural causes that have taken away their motivation and hope? There are individual poor people who are "lazy by nature"—as there are rich people—but surely we cannot sweep aside enormous sectors of the population with such a simplistic affirmation. The bulk of disadvantaged people work hard. Yet many fail to move up the social ladder.

For young people who arrive at this level of awareness, it is clear that God created people equal and that all should have the same opportunities. A poor child and a rich child do not face life with the same resources and the same opportunities. In its report in 1977, the Carnegie Council for Children affirmed that the most important factor that weighs against tens of millions of youth succeeding, in the United States, is poverty. In developing countries the situation is much more serious.

The lenses used do not depend necessarily on the position people occupy in the social pyramid. A very strange thing happens: many underprivileged people see reality through the lenses of the dominant class. The dominant ideology that justifies an unjust social organization can be interjected into the mind of the disadvantaged classes by the media, the educational system, the family, conversation, and even religion itself. Many disadvantaged people believe they are poor because of bad luck, destiny, or God's will, or because this is the natural organization of things. Thus the need for awareness raising or conscientization.

Many, especially those in third world countries, find themselves in a vicious circle of:

Unjust structures often determine the rules that the poor are obliged to follow. The rules govern access to power, resources, quality education, positions of authority, and the right to make decisions. The disadvantaged are in a game where the rules are largely made by the adversarial team. In such a game, we should not be surprised when some disadvantaged people become discouraged, are no longer interested in work, start drinking, or abandon their families. The success which stimulates other people is absent in everything they do. And so escape from bondage begins with the capacity to imagine that things can be other than they are.

On an international level there is also lack of equality between first and third world countries. Some argue that poor countries have only to imitate rich ones to progress. This was the dominant ideology of the 1960s. It is now seen to ignore important factors such as dependency of poor countries on rich countries. On an international level, economic structures of free marketing favor the exploitation of impoverished countries by industrially more advanced ones. An example is the rule of external debts that oblige poor countries to export billions of dollars annually to pay the interest on loans. The cost is high: the hunger and misery of the majority of their populations. The Latin American bishops have questioned the validity of this debt "when the payment means serious danger of survival for whole peoples, when the population was not consulted before contracting the debt, and when the latter was used for ends not always licit" (Puebla Document 197). For most countries, there is no light at the end of a dark tunnel unless the rules are changed.

Youth ministry in the United States—more than in any other country in the world—has a special obligation to deal with the international dimension of faith commitment. The United States, as a world power, is involved in the economic, cultural and political life of most other countries. Sometimes it is for their good; sometimes it is not. Sometimes, for example, the military who most oppress and exploit their people in third world countries have been trained and armed by first world governments and international business corporations.

f. Breakdown in Values. In modern society there is a

breakdown of basic values. There is a spiritual crisis. Selfishness and cynicism are the all-prevailing attitudes of many people. A culture of immediate gratification undermines attitudes of sacrifice and solidarity. In the United States there are over a million out-of-wedlock teenage pregnancies each year. Forty percent of all U.S. children are born into homes where there was never a marriage. Twenty-seven percent of all pregnancies end in abortion. Violent crimes committed by youth have spiraled out of control. Inner cities have been destroyed by crime. Garbage is thrown around without respect for the good of the community. There is no community. Gone are the neighborhoods where everyone looked after everyone else's kids. Few families escape the devastation wrought by drugs and alcohol. Educational standards have dropped alarmingly. The future of young people brought up in this environment is bleak indeed.

Today there is a worldwide awareness that if we fail to restore basic values, the fabric of society will be torn apart. This is a very positive development. In political elections, the restoration of traditional values has become a central matter. Though liberal groups have been responsible in the past for many social advances such as the end of slavery, the fight against segregation, the right of women to vote, the end of child labor, and the six day work-week, they have often failed to address the issue of values. They have dealt with economic oppression but largely ignored the need for meaning.

Conservative groups, on the other hand, lead a campaign to restore family values. Yet these groups champion an extreme type of market economics that is one of the principal causes of selfishness, materialism, and the breakdown of values in society. Their efforts to prevent government from interfering with the market allows the private sector to set up the rules that make it possible for them to maximize their profits, unhindered by laws that protect the environment, consumer health, safety standards and job security. The Irish bishops have pointed out that "uncontrolled and blind market forces favor the powerful and neglect the weak."[22] The breakdown in values is blamed on minority and disadvantaged groups, and the economic system that promotes a mentality of the survival of the fittest and the maximization of profits is ignored. Social policies favor powerful groups. Conservative groups have linked the issue of values to the need to dismantle the safety net for needy families. People are manipulated with simple answers to complex questions. While reform is often necessary, throwing people overboard and taking away their life jackets is unlikely to help them get back on their feet again. By punishing adults, children are also punished. And if we punish children, what sort of a future are we preparing? The solution for crime is seen in building more prisons and adding more police, rather than in dealing with the structural causes of crime: poverty and the influence of the mass media with its emphasis on sex, violence, and instant gratification.

But if we are defending family values we need to see where problems connect. We need to look at a serious aspect of the question: the effects of unemployment and poverty on family values. Conservative groups frequently ignore some of the deeper structural causes that provoke this breakdown of values: inability to cope emotionally due to economic pressures, less time spent with kids due to overwork, low wages, education, lack of jobs and job security. Special interest groups can afford a powerful lobby that gives them an advantage over the common citizen. Companies need to make a profit but they are also responsible for the welfare of the community. Many people are only two paychecks away from homelessness. Often the wages of non-skilled workers are not sufficient to motivate people to work and raise a family in a healthy environment. If we push people off a cliff can we blame them for not picking themselves up. While we cannot ignore individual responsibility for virtue, neither can we ignore the creation of an environment that makes virtue possible only for the heroic. The scapegoating and demonizing of the poor because of the ills of society has the result of driving a deeper wedge between the social classes. We divide rather than unite. We prepare a very ominous future when we push over the edge people who are barely coping. And demonizing the poor distracts people from seeing the massive transfer of wealth from other sectors of society to the top ten percent of the population.

Obviously one can go too far by blaming everything on structural causes and the influence of the environment. Personal responsibility must also be faced. We are equally unrealistic when we romanticize the poor.

But faith, as Teilhard de Chardin reminds us, is not a call to escape the world but to embrace it. Youth must be active participants in calling governments into accountability for all of its people, particularly Christ's poor and weak. Politicians need to be reminded that a country has a moral obligation to feed and protect those who cannot feed and protect themselves. It has an obligation to set a minimum standard for civilized society and raise the oppressed and the disadvantaged to that level. Government programs should not encourage laziness and dependency but rather help people to help themselves and help those who cannot help themselves. A strong country is a country where all its citizens go forward together. If all are to have equal opportunity, we need to level the playing field so that one side does not have to play uphill. President Lyndon Johnson used a forceful metaphor to describe the challenge: "You do not take a person who, for years, has been hobbled by chains and liberate him, bring him up to the starting line of a race and then say, 'You are free to compete with all the others,' and still justly believe that you have been completely fair."

Youth ministry needs to collaborate with other organizations in society in rebuilding neighborhoods and communities and promoting an environment that favors important values: solidarity, compassion, justice, and faith. In this effort to restore values to the society and build character, churches have an important role.

g. Flight by Preaching Abstract Values. Some pastoral ministries and movements remain on the level of preaching abstract values—love, fraternity, comprehension—without ever talking of the political forces in real life that can either promote or cancel these values. Such movements have a naive vision of society. They believe that all social classes and groups, especially Christians, are working for the common good of all. They speak of abstract values without analyzing the deeper causes that make these same values unfeasible in the concrete social organization. They are blissfully unaware of the existence of interest groups and the power they wield in determining the rules of social organization. Naive people fail to see the enormous influence these groups exercise over governments and politicians. Certain bills to better the quality of life of the majority are defeated in Congress because of the lobbying force of powerful interest groups. Even educated people can be naive due to more sophisticated control and manipulation by elite groups. Here we are not talking of the good or bad will of individuals. Although structures are created by human beings, once created they have the power to pressure people into certain behavior patterns.

And so youth ministry has to decide what side it is on in the conflict of different interest groups. And on which side is God in the bible?

h. Conflict Between Conflict and Love. The South African theologian Albert Nolan observes: "In some cases there is a structural conflict between rich and poor. This is not a personal quarrel. In these cases we cannot and should not blame the individuals involved, nor should we treat everybody on one side as innocent and everyone on the other side as guilty. Structurally the cause of the poor and oppressed is certain and just, independent of their personal and private lives. The cause of the rich and the oppressors is wrong, independent of the degree of awareness, honesty and sincerity."[23]

While Jesus said we should love our enemies, he did not say that we should avoid conflict and confrontation. He faced conflict in his own life. We love our enemies, but we seek their conversion. For love to be real, it may be necessary to thrust the scalpel into the tumors of social organization. Historically this is one of the ways social change has taken place. Awareness raising, organization, and pressure, at times, are important strategies for "bringing down the powerful from their thrones." This does not mean confrontation in the sense of hate and violence. The method of active nonviolence[24] would seem to be the option most coherent with the gospel. Martin Luther King, Jr. used the method with great efficiency to defeat discrimination, better educational opportunities, and gain political power for black Americans during the civil rights movement in the United States.

i. Contact with the Poor Is Fundamental. The youth from the middle and upper classes can also change their take on the perspective of those who are victims. This means showing solidarity with the cause of the disadvantaged groups in society. Work done with underprivileged youth must aim at making them subjects of their own destiny rather than keeping them in a state of dependency. Social change is possible only to the extent that marginalized people organize themselves and are empowered, with the help of idealistic people from other classes.

Contact with the conflict situation of the poor is essential to change the perspective of youth leaders. Simply listening to conferences on social problems rarely produces conversion. Changes in the church, in many countries, have taken place when church leaders moved from the perspective of elite groups to that of the poor. They took sides in the "noble struggle" of the impoverished for social justice. In many Latin American countries the church has suffered persecution and defamation as a result. This is the first time the predominantly Catholic continent has produced so many martyrs: laity, youth, priests, sisters, bishops. Hundreds have been assassinated not because they were distributing food, but because they pointed at structural causes of poverty. They were seen as a threat to the interests of the powerful.

Throughout history the church has chosen sides—sometimes the wrong side. Even today, the French church, for example, still suffers from the negative effects of its support for the king and the aristocracy during the French Revolution. The Anglican Church in England lost many of its faithful, especially the workers, through its association with the upper class during the industrial revolution. The church in Ireland was persecuted and so won the loyalty of an oppressed people. The church in the United States won the allegiance of Catholics by its support for the multitude of poor immigrants who arrived on its shores, in the past. It lost the African Americans by failing to be a prophetic voice against slavery and by arriving late in the civil rights movement. Increased material well-being of churches in the United States and in other first world countries place them again in danger of choosing the wrong side, of failing to read the signs of the times, of lack of courage in living the prophetic dimension of the gospel.

j. An Important Alert. We wish to issue an important alert here. The analysis of society in terms of conflict of interest groups helps us to understand the structural causes that create marginalization in the modern world. Interest groups with power and money have an enormous advantage in determining the rules of the economic and political game. As a method of analysis, however, we cannot make it an absolute. We have to avoid a reductionist analysis that is based only on economic factors and ignores other forces such as culture, subjective elements, religion, and politics. Using this method in an absolute way can lead to a Manichean view of the world, in which people are divided into two camps, the oppressors and the oppressed, the good and the bad, and where there are no undefined areas in the middle. Such analyses fall into the trap of over-simplification of the type: "all bosses are bad, all workers are good," "all rich people are bad, all poor people are good." Under the influence of such a simplistic vision young people rebel against exploitation but are not formed with a work ethic. They fail to take into account that people who exploit frequently do not see themselves as exploiters. Many sincere Christians, for example, think that "the poor are poor because they do not work." The question is not personal; it is structural. People may not have been brought to a certain level of awareness to be able to understand the real forces that shape the quality of life of people around them. They remain on the level of secondary and more visible causes only. When the conflictive model is used in an absolute way, common values are ignored. Analyses are frequently emotional and simplistic and fail to capture the complexity of social organization. People are labeled liberal or conservative, right wing or left wing, without an objective analysis of positions. Fatal mistakes are made when it comes to analyzing the relation of forces in society and the necessary coalitions that must be formed to bring about change. On the other hand, we cannot ignore that there are people who know they are exploiters and consciously put money and power above human solidarity.

This alert, however, should not be interpreted as an effort to diminish the importance of a conflictual analysis of society. Without this analysis, causes remain hidden and solutions proposed are mere palliatives. The alert is made so that the method may be used with greater scientific rigor.

k. Political Awareness. During the phase of writing this chapter, I presented an earlier draft to an important leader of youth ministry in the United States. He reminded me that most people understand politics to be that which takes place in Washington and has no influence on their lives. Politics is also associated with corruption and lies. I toyed with the idea of not using the term since it can evoke so many different meanings in people's minds, but then I remembered that one of the popes had said that political involvement is the noblest act of charity. Many church documents talk about the importance of Christian laity in political activity. Politics after all is where decisions are made that affect the quality of life of the entire population. So we need to recover the true meaning of this word. Many Christian youth can be very politically naive. This is hardly a virtue to be encouraged if youth ministry is to form leaders who are relevant in today's society.

Political involvement can be understood in the wider sense of concern for the "polis" (Greek word for city), the common good. Although the term includes party politics, it should not be reduced to this. The church does not make a party option, but will give young people civic and religious education so they can make their own options. In this sense not to be politically involved is not to be concerned with the common good. In places where it is not advisable to use the term "political" involvement, other terms can be used such as participation in public life or taking on the role of citizens in society. Jimmy Carter, on retiring as president of the United States, stated: "I now take up the only other function that is higher than president, that of citizen."

This stage emphasizes the political dimension of the faith. Young people now realize the importance of influencing political power if change is to take place. Young people who arrive at this level of awareness are able to recognize politicians who seek to mislead the people with enthusiastic discourses in favor of the disadvantaged while in practice defending the interests of powerful and narrow elite groups. They are able to unmask politicians who work against the interests of the majority.

The Fight for Justice. The young people now perceive that a youth ministry that is vague and undefined is going nowhere and will be unable to contribute to the solution of problems discussed. They perceive the limitations of the advice given by a priest to youth leaders: "What I really believe in is the ministry of a smile. It's nice to smile at a poor kid." One young person retorted: "This sort of sugary love is not going to solve our enormous social problems." The fight for justice is not something we can leave out of the religious formation of youth. The document, "Justice in the World" (Synod of Bishops, 1972) speaks of justice as a "constitutive dimension of the preaching of the gospel" (no. 6).

Brennan Hill suggests an interesting way of beginning: "At one time or another, everyone has experienced **unfair treatment.** It seldom takes long to remember such instances and even to feel again the hurt and resentment. It is useful to begin **education in justice** with reflection on such personal experiences."[25]

At this stage vital questions are discussed and studied: educational problems (quality of education, student organization), local neighborhood problems (housing, health, transport, isolation, lack of organization), work problems (unemployment, salaries, labor unions). Young people discuss politics, economics, and multinationals. The liberating power of the Christian faith comes to life as they see religion in a new way.

More conscientized groups may study the relation between economics, politics, ideology and religion. Bible study is no longer restricted to isolated texts. Importance is given to a systematic study of scripture through courses, conferences and reading. Experts are invited to help with a more intellectual, theological and sociological understanding of the surrounding society.

Young people now begin to take seriously the specific vocation of the laity to transform their environment. The challenge now is how to act. There is a temptation to think in terms of actions that mobilize many people and not give value to small actions: the continuous daily work of changing ideas, of mutual help, of conscientizing, of supporting the disadvantaged, of involvement in the parish community. All action, no matter how small, is transforming, to the extent that it is critically evaluated, within the context of a more global and structural vision of society. An Austrian youth minister put it this way: "We need to think globally and act locally." It does not matter how small the action once it is in the right direction. Global thinking is the guarantee of right direction, while local involvement avoids the futility of sterile discourses. If we think only globally the effect is paralyzing. Larger problems need to be subdivided into smaller units that can be administered more easily.

l. Religion Incarnated in the Happenings Around Us. Concern and action for justice is a characteristic of mature faith. Young people who pass to this stage of faith development have overcome the separation between faith and life. Religion is now seen not only as a Sunday morning activity, but as something that permeates all life. Celebrations that previously emphasized tranquillity, comfort and peace now begin to include a concern for social justice. Religion goes beyond the feeling of comfort and challenges the young person to take sides. The prophet Isaiah reminds us that "Peace is the fruit of justice" (Is 32:17).

There is now a wider and richer vision of church. The biblical theme of the "reign of God" now becomes central. The church is no longer seen as existing for itself. It exists for the mission—to build the reign of God. Everything that promotes justice and human dignity in society is a partial realization of this reign. Young people are clear that the gospel of the son of the carpenter must not be used again to legitimate systems that harm the disadvantaged. Neither should the church make alliances with the powerful in detriment to the cause of the poor—in exchange for privileges within the institution itself. The church needs to be a prophetic voice in modern society, even at the cost of losing privileges. To do otherwise is to be unfaithful to Christ's message and to risk being irrelevant in today's world.

m. Personal Conversion. When describing this stage of faith development we talked a lot of structural change and of structural sin. This is one side of the coin. The other side is personal conversion and personal sin. We must not put one up against the other: structural change or personal change. Both go together and are part of God's salvific plan. Some point to individual conversion as the only way to social change. This point of view ignores the fact that political, economic and cultural structures condition people's thinking, behavior and life-style. Transcendental meditation can bring peace to a few people but alone it has little influence over society's direction. It can be an escape from reality. On the other hand, structural change that is not accompanied by personal conversion changes very little. Interior cravings are left unanswered. It can in fact be a short-cut to producing new oppression, as history has frequently shown. The advice of scripture cannot be ignored: "First take the log out of your own eye, and then you will be able to see clearly to take the speck out of your brother's eye" (Mt 7:4-5).

The difficulty at this stage is to articulate the larger questions on the national and international level with the concerns and problems of daily life: family conflict, negative self-image, unemployment, alcoholic parent, friendship, dating, profession, religion, leisure, personal problems, etc. The temptation at this stage is to ignore the "stuff" of daily life. This was the error committed by many youth leaders in the 1960s. An option to work only on the structural level can form highly politicized leaders whose personal lives are a tragedy. Transformation that is not concerned with people's daily lives is not transformation. Neither is it a correct reading of the gospel message.

6. Discovery of Commitment

Young people at this stage widen their horizons to another dimension of life: commitment. It is the moment of saying "yes" to the Lord's call: "Come, follow me" (Mt 19:21) and "Go to all parts of the world and announce the good news to all creatures" (Mk 16:15). There is an important difference here. In previous stages young people would oscillate between bursts of enthusiasm, when taking on certain tasks, followed by moments of discouragement and irresponsibility.

However now the young people have been molded into leaders. They are persevering. Adverse circumstances are incapable of deterring them. Commitment no longer depends

on feelings of the moment. They have now embraced a life style that is permanent. They no longer want to be specta- tors, but have decided to go on to the field and play. A new awareness is summed up by one young person: "I cannot understand people who pass through this life and do nothing to change the place where they are." In every diocese we find young people at this level of dedication—the result of a long slow process of formation.

The young person is now coming to the end of an important stage of his or her faith journey, having come a long way from the initial stage. One youth leader remembers: "I entered the youth group to play games. Before I never thought about anything; I wasn't aware of the world; I shut myself up at home; I only studied and had a good time. Now I am committed to a cause that gives new purpose to my life." At this stage, young people are open to the world. A psychologist describes this growth process as a gradual but progressive amplification of the self to incorporate the world "outside." "As the person grows the frontiers of the self become more diluted. In this way, the more we extend ourselves, the more we love and the more diffuse becomes the distinction between the self and the world. And to the extent that the frontiers of our self become diffuse and diluted, we begin to experience the same emotion of ecstasy we feel when the frontiers of our self fall apart partially and we fall in love."[26]

The challenge for youth ministry is to help young people through the different stages until they become committed Christians. Many give up on the way because of lack of formation and systematic follow-up. However, formation involves a long process that can never be substituted by magical moments of emotion and enthusiasm.

a. Vocational Option. This is the stage of many religious and social options. It is the moment of passing from passivity to commitment. In religious terms we refer to this stage as one of vocational option. People listen to the call of the Lord and take on concrete commitments. The common vocation of all baptized Christians now becomes a reality to the extent that young people become involved in the parish community, in youth ministry or in some social commitment. "This rupture from passive apathy to initiative is considered by many as the central factor in the process of development."[27] It is the challenge of John Paul II to young people today: "The future depends on you. The end of this millennium and the beginning of the new depends on you. Don't be passive, therefore; seek to take on your responsibilities in all fields that are opened to you in this world!"[28]

b. Three Fields of Action. Young people have different gifts and skills. Some feel more attracted to commitment on the internal level of the church; others feel called to become involved in the struggle for social justice. Involvement can take place on three levels:

i) Internal Involvement Within the Youth Ministry Itself. Some young people give priority to youth work: preparing formation material, meetings, organizing courses, retreats, evaluation and planning sessions, music festivals, giving talks, forming new groups, visiting and accompanying young people in a systematic way. This type of commitment is important. Without the generosity and dedication of many youth leaders, youth ministry would disappear.

ii) Involvement in the Parish Community. Others give priority to working within the wider community, preparing adolescents for confirmation, giving religious education classes, participating in liturgical commissions, organizing the parish bulletin, organizing festivals, giving talks, directing local radio programs, coordinating reflection groups. In disadvantaged areas many of the leaders are young people since they are the most articulate and educated. Many creative liturgies are inspired by youth. Obviously we are talking here of churches that have undertaken a process of renewal. They work for the renewal of the church in view of its transforming mission in the world.

Youth ministry finds its identity through this awareness of a mission to be performed. Commitment in the church community is seen as related to the mission in society. Young people are often the first ones to insist that parishes be more relevant in the modern world. Many parishes are in a "state of coma" because they lack the dynamism and questioning spirit of the young.

This is the moment when vocations of special consecration come to maturity: vocations for the priesthood or religious life. This can bring a new challenge for our houses of formation that may be accustomed to dealing with more passive candidates. More open structures of participation are necessary for candidates who have previously exercised roles of leadership. It is also the moment when young people see the choice of the married state as a response to God's call to change the world.

In many places today there is a new generation of committed lay leaders, priests, brothers and sisters formed by youth ministry. They are bringing a new dynamism to the church. Through work with young people they have learned the skills of team work, the importance of an adult laity, and the need for solidarity with the disadvantaged.

iii) Involvement in Society. Young people at this stage also realize that society needs to be changed. The different organizations that bring people together in civil society are the privileged tools of change. Young people become involved in student organizations, grass roots movements, neighborhood organizations, programs among the poor, political parties, and labor unions. Organization and awareness raising are the keys to change.

The young people see this social involvement as a consequence of their faith. They recognize the Lord who is present, acts and saves, in the struggle of the poor. They take on the specific role of the Christian laity in the transformation of the world.[29] As lay people they are better equipped and have more credibility than priests and religious for this task.

In developing countries a new phenomenon is taking place. Manipulative and corrupt leadership—in politics, in labor unions, and in local organizations—are being substituted by more authentic leaders, many of them formed by different church ministries with a strong presence of young people. Youth ministry in the past was considered festive and superficial. Today, in many places it has gained credibility through the seriousness of its methodology, and by its ability to form committed leaders.

7. Discovery of Previous Stages

This last stage is the phase of pedagogical maturity. Youth leaders are now more realistic. They are aware that the evolution toward faith maturity and commitment is gradual. There are no "quick fixes." The youth leader needs patience above all. "Effective educators accept people where they are and then help them move from there by stimulating understanding and growth."[30] They avoid imposing their views and demanding the same level of commitment from beginners as from leaders. They can distinguish the stages of the young people they work with, respect these stages, and help the more courageous to face the challenge of more advanced stages. Care is taken not to confuse the desired-level-of-commitment with the possible-level-of-commitment. Youth leaders realize that the process of education in the faith is slow and different for each person. There are no magic formulas that can be applied in weekend courses or in meetings. Formation is a slow and long process.

This final stage may look easy but, in fact, it is one of the most difficult. Many young people who pass to the commitment stage are unable to take this further step. Although they themselves have passed through the different stages, they are often unaware of having done so. And so they find it hard to be patient with those who are putting their feet on the first rung of the ladder of commitment. They want the young people to commit themselves immediately. At times they use a more advanced jargon that is incomprehensible to beginners. In the words of one girl: "They want to give barbecued meat to a newly born infant and then wonder why it's gone into convulsions." At times they impose their ideas on a passive audience that has not yet acquired the intellectual clarity to be able to react. Their discourse can be one of liberation, but their pedagogy one of domination. As a result, the youth organization enters a phase of demobilization. Youth groups begin to distance themselves from coordination committees that have not yet acquired the wisdom and skills of this final stage.

The inability to arrive at this stage is a sure formula for isolation and lack of efficacy of coordination committees. The discovery of the previous stages leads to the development of mature committees who have excellent pedagogy.

4

Other Factors

OBSERVATIONS

A number of factors and observations need to be made on the passage through the different stages.

1. Growth Is Not Automatic. The passage from one stage to another is not automatic. Some people remain all their lives at the initial stages. Many abandon ship in the early stages. The passage to more demanding stages depends on the methodology used and the presence of competent adult advisors and youth leaders, whose style of Christian life is authentic and attractive to young people.

On the other hand, faith experience cannot be tied down to rigid chronological stages. Faith in the last analysis is a gift and the Spirit is free to act where, when and as he wishes. Nevertheless, we can and should prepare the ground so that the seed can germinate more easily. Faith comes, in the last analysis, from God; but God works in an incarnate way. The development of a mature faith depends on three factors: the grace of God, our personal options, and the environment we create.

2. Flexibility Between Stages. Education by stages does not mean necessarily a chronological process in which one stage follows another. Different stages can coincide. Young people with longer strides may also jump some of the steps. A young person, for example, may arrive at the stage of commitment, but without having passed through the stage of the discovery of structural causes. Another young person can take on strong social commitment without having passed through the discovery of the church community. The stages are a process that are more methodological than chronological. Neither should they be considered as separate. In real life situations, different stages can develop at the same time. The stages interpenetrate mutually; there are no clear dividing lines. We cannot decide the exact period of passage from one stage to another. Each person has his or her own personality and history and this should be respected.

Erik Erikson points out that previous stages continue operating when people advance to new ones. The new stage however receives the most attention and exercises the most influence. Westerhoff sees stages as styles of faith rather than steps ordered in a hierarchical and predictable fashion through which we pass in a sequential way.

3. Stages of Persons—Not of Groups. It is important to understand that the stages we have described are stages of the growth of persons—not of groups. Experience has shown that groups as a whole do not pass through the different stages of faith development. It is rather individuals within the group that develop, each at his or her own pace. So growth within a group is always unequal. Some advance more rapidly than others, in terms of commitment and critical awareness. There are a number of reasons for this phenomenon: young people come from different faith backgrounds, some are more idealistic, more generous than others, personalities are different, etc. So it's not possible to squeeze them all into the same educational program, as is frequently done with school catechesis.

4. Different Images. Images are stronger than words for communicating ideas with young people. Images work with the visual, with the emotions and with the imagination, and consequently the assimilation and retention of ideas are more lasting. We can use images of **steps, stairs or mountain climbing** to communicate the idea of challenge, of evolution, and the need to avoid stagnation on the faith journey. Each new stage is a challenge to grow. Challenge brings out the best in young people. Christ challenges his followers: "Be perfect, because your Father is perfect." When young people find themselves in a situation where there is no challenge—where "it is always the same old story"—they tend to leave and not return. This is the advantage of a proposal of development through stages. Instinctively the young person detects that to stop growing is to go backward. Each new stage is a new challenge that opens increasingly wider and richer horizons of faith and human growth.

Nevertheless, we have to avoid the notion of individual social climbing: the higher the better, the more perfect, the more superior to others. Mountain climbing involves team work and solidarity; it is not just the work of one individual. Those who are higher help pull up those who are underneath and those who are underneath push forward those climbing to a new level. All the climbers are attached and linked together by means of a common rope. If one slips, all the others risk their lives to keep him from perhaps falling to his death. Society proposes a relationship of competition to young people; here we propose a relationship of cooperation.

Two other images can complement the notion of steps: a) the image of a **spiral** and b) the image of **concentric circles**.

Image of a Spiral. The image of a spiral presents in a visual way an important truth: progress is not linear. There are moments of advance, of stagnation and even of retreat to a previous stage. There are "ups-and-downs" as we push forward on the road to success.

Concentric Circles. Stages can also be compared to concentric circles. As young persons outgrow the confining and restrictive limits of their present stage, they burst through these limits into a broader one. In stage development, new and wider horizons are continually being opened up as the young person pushes forward. Like a stone thrown into a lake, the circles expand in ever widening radii.

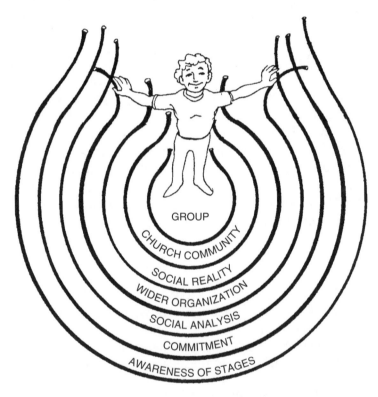

When young people enter a group, their focus is often on themselves. "In general, the mental frame work of each person is very limited and primitive, elaborated only around some basic needs. Persons live around two or three needs or values while ignoring the other possibilities of life."[31] Through group interaction young persons learn to understand the perspective of others and to understand their motivation. They learn to feel with and for the other person (what in psychology is called empathy). To the extent that young persons grow, this empathy extends beyond the group of friends and relations to the people who are in need of solidarity in the neighborhood, city, nation, and universe. Finally the growth process leads young persons to open their arms to all people—linked through a common humanity. For Christians, faith brings this universal unity to a more profound level: we are all brothers and sisters in Jesus Christ.

The study and assimilation of each stage offers new stimuli that propels young people forward to new horizons of commitment. The widening horizons of the mind bring a new joy to life.

Each stage builds on previous ones. New theory and experiences presented by youth leaders must be related to conscious and unconscious questions young people are asking. A basic pedagogical principle is followed: "The unknown can only be known by starting with the known." To teach John, I must first start with what John knows. In the stages of faith development, each stage has its questions that prepare the way for a new stage. Therefore, starting with the immediate and more superficial interests of young people, youth leaders focus on more altruistic interests, preparing the way for the ultimate questions that only religion can answer. This process continually creates expectations and interest—the principle of all motivation. The young person is enthusiastic and motivated to the extent that he or she has a feeling, not of stagnation, but of growth, of discovery of new worlds, of facing new challenges. This is the secret of all learning processes that aim at being liberating and successful.

5. Evolution of Faith. To the extent that the young person passes from one stage to another there is an evolution of the different elements of faith: God, prayer, Jesus Christ, church, bible, celebration, morality. The idea a child has of God, for example, is very distinct from the notion of a mature person. Those who do not evolve find it difficult to situate their faith in an increasingly intellectual and educated environment. The faith of a young person, whose notion of God is that of a child, for example, will hardly survive in the context of a modern secular university. A person who arrives at the commitment stage, on the other hand, will have a more liberating and incarnated notion of the church, of God, of Jesus Christ, of the bible, than when he or she started out on the faith journey.

6. Continuous Decrease of Numbers. As the young people in the group pass through different stages, the number of participants diminish. At the beginning there is larger number of participants since the focus is on personal relations. A smaller number remain, as further stages demand more reflection and commitment. This was the experience of Jesus himself when some of his disciples found his challenge too demanding: "Many of his followers heard this and said: 'This teaching is too hard. Who can listen to it?'...Because of this, many of Jesus' followers turned back and would not go with him anymore" (Jn 6:60-66). So we should not be disappointed because some drop out on the way. Youth ministry aims at forming leaders; leaders are few, but they are precious. A small nucleus of leaders is to be found leading the majority of social, political and religious activities. They are the committed people who involve and mobilize the masses.

7. Different Youth Ministries. When we described the stages, we talked more of parish youth groups. But the pedagogy of stages can be applied also to specialized youth ministry: groups of high school kids, university students, worker youth, rural youth, and youth at risk (drugs, street gangs, etc.). The type of group will determine the necessary adaptations. A university group, for example, will have a different way of dealing with the question of integration in a church community (second stage: discovery of community), and a parish community may not be the only option.

8. Stages as a Tool for Evaluating. Stages of faith development can be a useful tool for evaluating the progress of a particular group or pastoral ministry. The vision of stages can help us pinpoint where young people are on the faith journey and detect the steps yet to be taken. A united effort between apostolic movements and youth ministry is now easier. A movement may bring a young person to certain stages. And this is positive. Perhaps other pastoral ministries and movements have the task of bringing the more questioning youth through more advanced stages.

9. Don't Give a Talk. A theory of youth ministry will indicate the correct goal (vision), which in turn will indicate the correct path to be taken (methodology). However stages are discovered. Resist the temptation to give a talk on the stages of development to **beginners.** The faith journey is not so simple. To give a talk would be to fall into the trap of the traditional deductive model. Beginners do not start by studying theory. At the beginning, each member of the group has his or her own goals and expectations. There is as yet no common goal. Goals have to be discussed and discovered together. Gradually individual goals are modified and a group goal comes into focus. However, someone in the group—normally the youth leader or youth minister—needs to **have the clarity that comes from a clear theory** of youth ministry; otherwise the blind will be leading the blind and "both will fall into the same ditch" (Lk 6:39). Many groups are in crisis because youth leaders have no clear theory of youth ministry, especially of stage development.

10. Adolescents and Young Adults. The stages of faith development must also take into account the age group we are dealing with: adolescents or young adults. Ideally adolescents should have opportunities to meet on their own, while at the same time participating in a wider youth ministry. These opportunities can be groups of adolescents, encounters for adolescents. An understanding of the special phase in the young person's life is a condition for working with this age group. (Cf. special characteristics of adolescents and young adults in Appendix A.)

FACTORS THAT FACILITATE GROWTH IN STAGES

1. Identification. In an age of great pluralism of models and ideas, the Christian message is assimilated by young people especially through a process known as identification. The determining factor in youth formation is the contact and identification with other young people, with adult youth ministers, with church organizations, with youth groups, with youth ministry, with small communities, with the parish—people and organizations that have a different life style from the surrounding society. These encounters between people are spaces where members radiate a different spirit. There a spirit of joy, enthusiasm, love, pardon, service, zeal for justice, solidarity with the disadvantaged, and confidence in the workings of the Holy Spirit. In these alternative environments, the young person has models that can be decisive in determining identity and interior unity.

We are not talking here of purely rational contact, of presenting convincing arguments and ideas. The religious experience is a holistic experience where the rational, the emotional, and the imagination are present. "Feeling well" in a community, at times, can be more important than the theological ideas discussed. It is this set of sensations, of living something that gives deep meaning to life, that fires many to bring the good news to others.

2. Importance of Success. Beginners have shallow roots that can easily be uprooted by adverse winds, by sudden storms. They need special support. The newly planted tree must be nourished if it is to survive. It is important that beginners have an experience of success in the activities that they are promoting. This means viable goals, good leadership, and good preparation to guarantee the quality of programs. The quality of a group meeting is fundamental. In some situations young people get most of their formation in group meetings. Success is fundamental. In a losing situation the tendency is to abandon what is perceived as a sinking ship. Success stimulates self-confidence and the conviction that change is possible.

Leaders, on the other hand, need to be more persistent than beginners. A leader who gives up easily is not a leader. A leader must be able to deal with failure and bounce back. Christ reminds us that the grain of wheat must first die in order to give fruit. There are no short-cuts without hard work. The difference between beginners and leaders is in their attitude to failure. Beginners drop out; leaders become more determined.

3. Leadership Formation. Groups may fall apart on the journey. At least four factors are responsible for their failure:

- lack of good youth leadership
- lack of preparation
- lack of method
- lack of adult advisors

4. Holistic Formation. Conditions for holistic formation need to be created as young people pass through different stages of faith development and critical awareness. A balance is sought between different dimensions of the young person's life:

- Self-knowledge (relationship with self)
- Integration (relationship with others)
- Social formation (relationship with society)
- Spiritual and theological formation (relationship with God)
- Leadership skills (tools for change)

5. Specialized Support Structures. A youth ministry that depends only on volunteers who study and work will find it difficult to advance. Leaders have very little time for a pastoral ministry that demands great dedication. More permanent structures with full-time youth workers are emerging in some countries: youth centers, youth institutes, centers for publication and distribution of formation material, and youth newspaper.

6. Youth Rallies. The work of small groups and of leadership training needs to be complemented with moments of mobilization of the masses of young people. Large concentrations of youth are important for animating the difficult task of everyday youth work. Youth rallies make youth ministry visible; credibility is increased. Some countries organize a national youth day for this purpose. In the United States the National Federation for Catholic Youth Ministry (NFCYM) organizes a national youth conference with an average of seven thousand participants. On the diocesan or parish level different formulas are used to mobilize the youth: celebrations, marches, shows, musical festivals, theater, rallies where young people are given the opportunity to address other young people. The International Youth Day is an example of this type of rally. In the international rally in Denver, in 1993, one young person commented: "Sometimes it's lonely being a Catholic. But here when I looked around I could see thousands who believe as I believe. This has given me new strength."

7. See–Judge–Act Method. The see-judge-act method has a central role in this model. It is an inductive transforming methodology that:

a) SEE: Starts with reality by asking for and discussing concrete facts and happenings in young people's lives.
b) JUDGE: The problems and challenges that emerge from this discussion are then confronted with gospel values.
c) ACT: Problems discussed are then acted upon. Action becomes an important part of formation. Doing becomes an important way of learning.

The codification of this method by Cardinal Cardijn and the young people of Specialized Catholic Action, during the initial half of this century, introduced a new way of working with young people. It also helped develop a spirituality appropriate to an urban and industrial age. The method brings an awareness to young people of their surrounding environment. As a method of formation it avoids abstract definitions. Its starting point are facts, concrete cases; from symptoms it moves to deeper causes; it analyzes the situation discussed in the light of the gospel and afterward moves to a change of attitudes and concrete action. Vatican II praised this method of formation, and the church in Latin America uses it for the majority of its documents and pastoral activities. The see-judge-act method has become the principal method of youth ministry and of many other pastoral ministries in Latin America.[32] It is not however the only method used.

The method brings out an important truth: faith develops and matures only in concrete life situations. Faith development involves the transformation of people and social structures. And so we present the proposal of Jesus as the answer to the concrete questions of youth, in a process in which action and reflection go together. God is present in the action. Only by starting with life experiences can we really understand the demands of the bible.

Commitment and action exercise an important role in the formation of youth. Specialized Catholic Action talked of "formation through action." A ministry that limits its goals to study and courses rarely produces real commitment or conversion. On the other hand, action without reflection leads to activism. Theoretical formation and practical commitment need to walk hand in hand on the road to genuine maturity.

This model accentuates the importance of social commitment and the formation of Christians who are subjects rather than objects of human history.

8. Interaction Theory/Praxis Method. As the see-judge-act method does not adequately take account of the place of theory, it needs to be complemented by the interaction method of theory/praxis. This method has as its basis the see-judge-act method and can be understood as an evolution of this method. The method makes clear the role of theory in formation.

Praxis can be understood as equivalent to the see-judge-act method. The praxis accentuates the importance of reflecting on what is going on around us. In order to reflect in an organized way a method is needed, in this case the see-judge-act method. The contrary of praxis is activism where there is an absence of reflection. Activism has little formative value. The Greek philosopher Plato reminds us that the unreflecting life is not worth living.

Relation to Theory. Theory is related to praxis. There is a continuous coming-and-going between theory and praxis. Theological, psychological and social theory are important for better understanding of the problems faced by youth. The praxis creates the need for theory while at the same time uncovering unconscious and hidden theories that lurk behind much of harmful human behavior. Praxis, for example, uncovers the hidden agenda of conservative theories that serve to cover over unjust situations or progressive theories that are unrealistic.

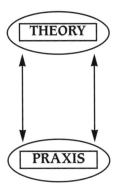

This theory/praxis method is used in group meetings, courses, elaboration of formation material, etc. This method avoids two extremes: on one side, a ministry that is limited to courses and study, and, on the other hand, a ministry of activities without any theoretical formation.

In this model, however, theoretical formation cannot depend on the whim of the moment. Neither can it depend on a spontaneous process that waits for the young people to manifest their desire for greater theoretical formation in a particular area. Education in stages must be supported by an annual planning process that includes courses, retreats, and formation material. A well-conducted evaluation will point to the activities to be programmed for the year. Once this process is launched it has its own dynamic, at times taking unforeseen directions. New horizons and new frontiers are continually opened. And this is the richness of the method.

CONCLUSION

In this chapter we have attempted to clarify the importance of stages in faith development for young people. While a knowledge of these stages is not necessary for beginners, it is an essential requirement for those who are leading youth ministry. Otherwise leaders are commanding an expedition in a strange land—without a road map.

Without a vision of stages of development there can be no focus and no priorities. Everything is given the same importance—and when everything is important, then nothing is important. Youth ministry becomes irrelevant. A vision of stages avoids out-of-touch leadership. The more advanced members learn to have patience with beginners while at the same time being challenged themselves to push forward. A vision of stages answers the burning question for all youth leaders: how to get from here to there, how to get from indifference to commitment and conversion.

When I had written this chapter I gave it to a nationally known expert in youth ministry in the United States. His principal concern was that readers would pick on the idea of stages of development as a magic solution for all the ills of youth ministry and neglect other important strategies. That is also my concern. An understanding of stages of development in both human and religious growth is one of the important strategies for developing an effective youth ministry. It has to be complemented, however, by a host of other strategies such as courses, seminars, encounters, retreats, assemblies, seminars, workshops, mass rallies, celebrations, prayer vigils, small group ministry, ministry to families, theater, sporting events, leadership training, systematic follow-up, organizational structures, pastoral planning, social and religious commitment, and formation through action. Stages are more a vision of where we want to arrive—our short and long term goals. They are the **"where"** but not the **"how."**

QUESTIONS FOR GROUP MEETINGS

1. Individual study of text (preferably before the meeting)

2. Sharing in group or groups

   Questions:
   i) What is the stage that corresponds to your own faith journey? What are the influences that helped you arrive at your present level of commitment?
   ii) At what stage are the other youth I work with—in my group or coordination committee?
   iii) What are the gaps and omissions on diocesan and parish levels? What can we do to correct them?
   iv) How can this vision of growth through stages of faith strengthen our youth ministry.
   v) How can we help young people to pass on to new stages in the faith journey?

Appendices

APPENDIX A:
SPECIAL CHARACTERISTICS OF
ADOLESCENTS AND YOUNG ADULTS

1. Adolescents

General Description: Adolescence can be extended from the ages of twelve to eighteen. The age can vary depending on the country, the social class, degree of responsibility, surrounding universe of affection, and level of education. This period is characterized by very rapid physical growth, sexual explosion, and acute sensitivity in face of approval or disapproval. The peer group has special importance. It seems that adolescents need to solve in a positive way their relationship with other young people before they can face the challenge of relating to adults and especially to their families. "Belonging to a group facilitates the psychological growth of the individual and serves as a force of integration...in early adolescence."[33]

Moral Development: Adolescents are passing through important stages of moral development. Lawrence Kohlberg[34] is perhaps the best known expert in this field. Kohlberg has shown that there is an evolution of moral reasoning. While stages 1 and 2 refer to childhood, stages 3, 4 and 5 have special importance for youth work.

Stage 3: Moral code based on the authority of others
Stage 4: Critical evaluation of this code
Stage 5: Personal moral code

STAGE 3: Moral Code Based on the Authority of Others. The majority of adolescents are at stage 3. This stage has special characteristics. The judgment of what is right and wrong is determined largely by pressures and expectations of people whom youth admire (other youth, family, adults, people in youth ministry, a priest, a sister, a teacher, etc. Adolescents comply with the state of things around them and may even seek to justify and defend the established order. Here, "there is an orientation in the direction of authority, fixed rules, and the upholding of the social order for its own sake."[35] At this stage morality is determined by a reference group. The problem is that when young people move from this group into a context with different values, this reference group loses its power.

The importance of an understanding of this phenomenon is illustrated by an experiment made by parish catechists. The team of catechists decided to change the minimum age for confirmation, from the age of twelve to eighteen, with the idea of bringing in more mature youth. The preparation course had previously attracted more than eighty adolescents annually. With the change only two young people over the age of eighteen came. It was too late. The young people at this age were already in the midst of a crisis provoked by the next stage (stage 4: critical evaluation of moral code). They were no longer open to encouragement or pressure from parents. Their ideas and behavior patterns were becoming more rigid. This would seem to vindicate strongly the importance of work with adolescence as a foundation for later work with older youth. A more tranquil and balanced passage through the turbulence of stage 4 is also possible when solid foundations are laid in stage 3. An understanding of this stage also helps us revise a commonly held belief that adolescents automatically question the existing order and easily assimilate a more political dimension of the faith.

STAGE 4: Critical Evaluation of This Code. But some adolescents may evolve to stage 4 of moral reasoning. At this stage rules and norms are re-evaluated and questioned. Adolescents are now able to deal with abstract ideas, to have their own opinions, to disagree with parents and other adults. They are now capable of working with universal values. They perceive the falsehood and incoherence of many models around them. There is now a rejection of authority and of everything that "comes from above." There is a period of self-affirmation, of emotional swings from euphoria to pessimism. Laws and rules of society are no longer accepted on the authority of others. The questioning of social rules does not mean their complete rejection. The questioning is a sign that the process of internalizing is taking place, thus forming the basis for the future development of moral reasoning. This process of inner motivation and judgment on moral issues has been traditionally termed conscience.

2. Young Adults

General Description. The phase of young adults starts around eighteen years of age, although for some it may start at sixteen. While young adults may still have characteristics of adolescence, they also find themselves at a stage of greater emotional balance and experience. Life has started to teach them the folly of over-simplification of complex issues. There are no black and white situations; gray areas have to be considered. Young people are less aggressive as they now have greater self-confidence. The period is characterized by a certain autonomy in relation to family; personal identity now becomes more solidified. Identity has been established through a process of crisis, re-evaluation, questioning and assimilation of a frame of reference and of values that give meaning and direction to life. This new value system has a function somewhat similar to the control panel of an airplane. Without the control panel the pilot has no direction. At this stage young people need to finish the building of their own control panel, their own frame of reference, their own value system. Otherwise life has no meaning, and no direction.

Personal identity is achieved, in general through experimentation with different roles. Young people experiment with different images of themselves until they decide on the one that best suits.

The capability of the young person to resolve the identity problem will depend on personal resources and support from family, school, youth ministers and the culture of the peer group.[36] For Erikson the identity crisis should be sufficiently resolved to make possible adult commitments of solidarity and mutual concern. Fowler claims that two further experiences are important if the young person is to achieve coherent and consistent moral reasoning: "In the first place, the young person should leave home emotionally and perhaps physically, and have experience of conflicting values in a moral context of moratoria [postponement]."[37] Then, "the young person...should take two further steps...the experience of feeling responsible for the welfare of others and the experience of taking on and living with irreversible moral options."[38] Scarcity of material resources can force some young people to take on these responsibilities early in life.

At the end of this stage, the young people should have the capacity to survive alone in a complex culture. They should have an integrated identity that includes the definition of themselves as sexual, moral and political participants. The development of identity represents a commitment to specific values that serve as a basis for future life decisions.[39] The young people who fail to establish their identity remain confused and dependent on others. One girl evaluated the egoist behavior of a colleague: "I pity him. He is wasting his life. He is more than twenty years of age and still hasn't a life-project."

Stages of Moral Development Among Young Adults.[40] During the phase of young adulthood there is a critical evaluation of the traditional moral code as the young people begin to question external morality (Stage 4: critical evaluation of moral code). Adults are often shocked by the rejection of traditional moral principles that are seen as oppressive and the product of backward ages. However, young people need to pass through this period of re-evaluation to arrive at a moral code that is personal and no longer depends on the authority of others. They need to question traditional moral principles. They need a new system of values to guide their behavior in a pluralistic society. I once accompanied youth leaders who were passing through this phase. Adults in the church were shocked (I was also upset) when they wrote an article in the youth newspaper rejecting marriage and defending sexual promiscuity. Despite strong criticism they refused to change their position. They agreed, however, to form a group to study the question. During several meetings they evolved from a phase of "knocking" church teaching to a phase of building a more mature moral code. In one meeting a girl remarked: "Life is more complex than we thought at first. We are leaving out important dimensions of the human person. There is more to the human person than the biological." Today, most of this group are happily married. They are now fathers and mothers of families—preparing themselves for the questionings that will soon come from their own children.

An understanding of the evolution of moral reasoning is important for those who work with young people. Young leaders themselves can understand their own interior drama and the drama of the young people they are guiding. Adults also discover the folly of making demands on youth that are psychologically impossible. Many adults in the church (laity, sisters, priests, brothers, bishops) commit the error of treating young people as adults and not taking into account the interior confusion that they face as adolescents and young adults. During this phase, young people are more in need of a hand extended in welcome and support than a hand raised to censure and condemnation.

STAGE 5: Personal Moral Code. An important characteristic of this phase of young adulthood is the development of a personal moral code—of the capacity for moral reasoning. This is the stage of mature morality. At this moment young people are building a moral code from personal convictions rather than from obedience to authority. This code is the result of questioning and re-evaluation of traditional moral principles in the light of new experience, new information and a new cultural context. Law is considered important, but not absolute. Outdated and unjust laws need to be changed. Unfortunately many young people in modern society do not make it across a shaky, swinging bridge to the stage of mature moral reasoning.

Important conclusions can be drawn for the different stages of our **community and social model.** The age bracket we are dealing with has to be considered. We need to recognize the emphasis on "received-faith" during adolescence (12–18) and the search for an "owned-faith" during the later phase of young adulthood (can start at 16). The temptation to maintain youth in the "hot house" atmosphere of the "received-faith" must be avoided. The future of the church and the building of God's reign depends on Christians who have already passed from the phase of "cultural Christians" to one in which the option to belong to a faith community is personal.

APPENDIX B:
STAGES OF FAITH DEVELOPMENT
ELABORATED BY FOWLER[41]

James Fowler is perhaps the most widely known theologian today who has studied the stages of faith development. His theory, in my view, can be understood not as an alternative to our community and social model, but rather as complementing it. It offers insights that enrich the understanding of this latter model. His theories were elaborated from surveys and academic work in which he incorporated discoveries of intellectuals such as Piaget, Erikson, and Kohlberg. Fowler distinguishes six stages. The stages are chronological and related to one another. Each stage incorporates elements of previous stages while adding new ones. The transition to a new stage begins as the person becomes aware of the limitations of the present stage. His theory seeks to integrate the rational approach with the emotional, the symbolic, the imagination.

Through in-depth interviews Fowler was able to start with experience and discern patterns in the stories of more than four hundred people. But because his theory does not come out of a pastoral context its application in a practical vein is difficult. Fowler's terminology is also very difficult. The stages of our community and social model, on the other hand, were elaborated in the context of the youth work itself and tested during more than fifteen years. They are, in my view, more functional as they came out of a pastoral experience. I have given many courses on this model. After a talk I usually divide people into groups and ask them to relate the stages of their own faith journey and that of their group.

More committed young people immediately locate the stages through which they have passed and with facility indicate the stages of the youth with whom they work. They will often remark that the absence of this theoretical understanding led them to commit many errors and to lose many members on the way.

For Fowler, the more common meaning of faith as belief in a personal and transcendent divinity is substituted for faith in the sense of fundamental attitude. Human faith can be a pre-condition for religious faith. Despite these shortcomings Fowler's work offers us some valuable insights that can complement our community and social model.

In Stage 1, which ends around six years of age, the child receives the faith of the parents in a very informal way, by imitating the religious attitudes of parents. In Stage 2, faith is transmitted through stories that have Christian attitudes and beliefs embodied in them. But we are really interested here in the subsequent third, fourth and fifth stages as these throw light on our pastoral work with youth. As Fowler uses a very complex terminology—not easily understood by young people—I have changed the names of the stages to make them more immediately intelligible:

Stage 3: Cultural faith
Stage 4: Personal faith
Stage 5: Mature faith

Stage 3: Cultural Faith. This stage corresponds to the "received faith" of Westerhoff that we have analyzed previously. It is the faith especially at the beginning of adolescence. The young person enters this stage of faith evolution, in general, around eleven or twelve years of age, when a person's experience is extended beyond the family and group of friends. At this stage the adolescent believes because of the religion and community in which he or she was born. There is a certain emotional solidarity with the group or community and an acceptance without questioning of authority figures. The young person believes because of others without examining the reasons for believing. There is as yet no personal faith. This type of faith depends a lot on a Catholic or traditional culture in which family, friends and acquaintances are practicing Christians. The stage begins with adolescence and for many people can last for the rest of their lives. Before the 1960s this was the last stage reached by the majority of people. In the past, this was the only stage envisioned by religious education, as we have seen when discussing the traditional deductive model. Formation was given by means of a catechism of questions and answers. And it worked. It worked because the culture was a traditional and Christian culture. This stage should not now be despised. It can still nourish a profound faith and confidence in God. It is the faith of many of our parents and grandparents. It can also serve as a basis for the next stage.

This type of faith, however, enters into crisis when the traditional culture changes to a modern culture. The people most affected are young people. This is the case, for example, of a young person who moves out from the family into a pluralistic environment: school, university, peer group, large city. In the new environment, cultural support for continuing to practice religion no longer exists. Now to be a Christian means to swim against the current.

So the third stage can no longer function as the final stage. Today, in general, it is a transition stage for the fourth stage (personal faith). The beginning of adolescence then, should be a preparation for the great adventure of transition to the fourth stage. Conditions need to be created in the third stage (cultural faith) so the young people may have an experience of sincere friendship, an environment of affection and support, space where they are protagonists, contact with Jesus as a friend, contact with people who suffer, appreciation for the bible related to life experience, experience of creative and meaningful celebrations. Only in this way will they have built a solid platform for securely launching them through the stormy phase of the fourth stage.

In general young people in the first four stages of the community and social model (group, community, social problem, wider organization) are at Fowler's third stage. His observations help us to understand and work with young people in these early stages.

Stage 4: Personal Faith. This stage corresponds to the stage of "faith owned" of Westerhoff that we have previously described. This fourth stage is the stage of personal faith and critical consciousness of the surrounding social environment. Young people are able to stand on their own feet; they no longer need the crutches of the third stage. For some young people this stage starts between the ages of sixteen and eighteen for others it starts only after thirty, for others after forty. And many people die without having made this step.

The fourth stage encourages personal faith, while building on the community values of the previous stage. In the third stage the young people are restricted to the values of the group in which they were born. The fourth stage is the moment of opening up their vision. They widen their vision, become aware of their own ideology and are able to understand other ideologies and points of view. They are concerned with poverty and suffering in the world. The political dimension of faith now becomes important, especially in third world countries where social contradictions are more accentuated. In first world countries there are also social problems, although to a lesser degree. Within this vision the struggle for social justice takes on an important role. The young people begin to reflect on the causes of the many economic, political, social and religious problems. They become aware of the influence of the rules, laws and structures of society on interpersonal relations and on social problems. They discover that the laws are not applied in the same way to rich and poor. They begin to think in terms of structural change. People who are oppressed in the third stage don't react. They can be very naive. They continue supporting unjust structural causes while at the same time praying that the symptoms will disappear. "The identity of people in the third stage is so tied in with the 'status quo' that it would be a form of psychic suicide to attack a system that is seen as the foundation of their existence. It is only in the fourth stage that the possibility of structural change becomes a viable solution."[42] This is the stage of critical consciousness and of a faith that goes beyond personal concerns and the immediate group of friends and relations.

At this stage, also, there is a questioning of a naive interpretation of doctrine and of the power of religious symbols. The relevance of religion is questioned. Simultaneously there is a search for an understanding of religion that can coexist with a scientific mentality: a synthesis between faith and science. It is the phase of the "whys" and strong statements: "Why should I believe?" "Why should I go to church?" Pressure from parents is no longer a sufficient motive for believing. A cultural faith that depends on the authority of others is now questioned. Just as morality was questioned, so also faith is questioned. Being a Christian because of family or community is seen as something negative. The search of the young person for a personal faith must first pass through a period of crisis and questioning that can have two consequences: abandonment of the faith or a maturation process in which faith is now accepted as personal. During this crisis there is a strong tendency to see the world in terms of "black-and-white." Instead of seeking a balanced view they often choose one of the two poles: social involvement or prayer divorced from any social commitment. At times, too, the intellectual dimension is accentuated and the affections are given little importance. The young people who previously lived an unquestioning relationship with God now enter into crisis. Doctrine is questioned. There is a rejection of religious symbols present, especially in the liturgy. The "rational phase" is not yet capable of understanding and including the symbolic world as one of the important aspects of human living. At the same time, the young people themselves are unaware of what is taking place. They are not aware that the crisis can be a process of faith maturation. Consequently, there are feelings of loss, of guilt, of affliction. The support of a youth minister can be an important factor in helping young people through this agitated passage. Without support the crisis can lead to abandonment of the faith.

The fourth stage of Fowler coincides with the discovery of structural causes (community and social model). It is the beginning of a critical awareness. His observations can help us to understand certain phenomena such as the "black-and-white" phase and vanguard attitudes of many youth leaders during this difficult period. It also helps us to perceive the enormous possibilities in terms of faith and commitment during this phase.

Stage 5: Mature Faith. In the fifth stage of maturity people have already moved out from the "black-or-white" phase. They are able to perceive positive values in apparently opposite poles, as, for example, prayer and social involvement, love of self and love of neighbor. Now the faith enters a new phase of integration. There is a more personal relationship with Christ and peace of spirit. Symbols take on a new meaning as they help in the understanding of life, while pointing to realities that go beyond the rational. Symbols express perceptions, emotions, experiences or intuitions that the intellect is incapable of reaching.

In the community and social model, the transition to more mature faith (fifth stage of Fowler) begins with the stages of discovery of commitment and previous stages). Fowler works with the stages of faith development during the whole life of the person—from birth until death. The community and social model, on the other hand, is more concerned with the age group touched by youth ministry. Therefore we cannot affirm that the last stage (discovery of previous stages) necessarily corresponds to the arrival at faith maturity. Fowler makes an observation which could change much of adult expectations about the young people they work with—making them more realistic. According to him the fifth stage of mature faith is not possible for adolescents as they have to deal with many specific problems of their age group: transition to adult life, identity crisis, self-discovery, emotional maturity, elaboration of their own value system, etc. If Fowler is right, this transition is only possible around twenty years of age or often much later. The observation has important implications for our work in youth ministry. Our expectations need to be more realistic to avoid unnecessary deceptions. We have to accept that before twenty years of age, our aim should be to help the young person to grow in personal relationship with Christ, acquire critical awareness of the world and take on some commitment in the church community or in society, but not to expect a level of faith maturity that may not be possible at this age.

Comments

The surveys done by Fowler indicate that the majority of people get "stuck" in the third stage of faith evolution (cultural faith). They arrive at the end of life without having advanced to subsequent stages. Some young people are afraid to step on the tightrope that passes over the turbulent waters of the fourth stage of personal faith. They prefer the security of the womb of the third stage to the birth pains of a new and unknown world. Some may take refuge in conservative movements or in fundamentalist sects where others will tell them what to do and how they can avoid the pain of thinking for themselves. This type of refuge, however, becomes increasingly vulnerable under the fire power of the piercing weapons of modern culture: the electronic means of communication. Unfortunately many institutions in the church still feel more tranquil with young people in the third stage and are reluctant to support the transition to a more mature faith (fourth stage). It is easier to deal with naive young people than with people who can think for themselves.

Faced with a shortage of vocations, some congregations are tempted to work only with young people from the third stage and keep them in a hothouse environment where they are protected from the challenges of the fourth stage. Immediate results are possible; long term results are questionable.

APPENDIX C:
SUMMARY OF STAGES OF FAITH DEVELOPMENT IN YOUTH MINISTRY

7. Discovery of Previous Stages
(Pedagogical Maturity)
6. Discovery of Commitment
(Vocational Option)
5. Discovery of Structural Causes
(Social Analysis)
4. Discovery of Need for a Wider Organization
3. Discovery of the Social Problem
2. Discovery of the Community
1. Discovery of the Group

The following is a resume of each stage:

1. Discovery of the Group

The young person needs a unit larger than the family, but not so large that he has the feeling of being a mere number in a crowd (as sometimes happens in a parish). He makes the first step by joining a group. The group serves as a bridge between the family and a world that often appears threatening. His vision widens to include more community aspects of life: team work, self-knowledge, capacity to relate to others. The gospel and the person of Jesus Christ are understood and accepted in a new way. Young people are encouraged to integrate gospel values into a personal, intellectual and social growth process. In an atmosphere of affection, faith is perceived as forming a frame of reference for the new identity that is being established. Faith gives a deeper meaning to life.

2. The Discovery of the Community

This stage challenges the group to broaden its horizons. Young people push forward and burst the restricted circle of the group. The group opens out to the wider reality of the parish community. They become enthusiastic with the discovery of a community model of church that is attuned to their own ideas. A sense of belonging-to-the-church is cultivated through an experience of church as a living community rather than by abstract study. The sense-of-belonging-to-the-church matures in somewhat the same way as emotional bonds of belonging to a family. Both an experiential and a theological understanding of the church are explored.

3. Discovery of the Social Problem

Now the horizon of the local church community has become too limiting. This circle is now ruptured and young people burst into a new world of experience: the drama of surrounding society. Who is my neighbor?—the central message of Jesus—is now the perturbing question that needs to be grappled with in meetings, talks and courses. The bible comes to life. Young people become involved in service programs to disadvantaged people. In this third stage, young people's vision of the social problem is still descriptive and naive and actions aim at eliminating effects rather than causes. Problems are considered in isolation. There is, as yet, no global or structural vision of society.

4. Discovery of a Wider Organization

This stage occurs when the young people move beyond their group and community and maintain contact with the wider youth organization. They discover "youth ministry."

Their group is no longer isolated. Many other groups, with the same ideals, are going in the same direction. Their influence and strength increase to the extent they are part of a wider youth organization. They now have a powerful voice within the church. Youth power has been harnessed for transformation.

In meetings, courses and assemblies young people evangelize other young people by their example of faith and dedication, by their commitment and action, through their talks and contributions in discussions. There are no better evangelizers of young people than their own companions. At this stage the vision of church is no longer restricted to the territorial limits of a parish. An awareness of the universal church and a perception of a living, vibrant organization, of a faith incarnated in real life situations, grows.

5. Discovery of Structural Causes

Now young people have conditions for making another step to expand the horizon of their world vision. This stage calls attention to an important task of youth ministry: the creation of critical awareness in today's world. Concern and action for justice is a characteristic of mature faith. Unjust structures shape people's thinking and values and create poverty and marginalization. Action must be preceded by an analysis of causes to avoid attending to the fever while ignoring the infection—of giving an aspirin to cure an appendix. Young people who pass to this stage of faith development have overcome the separation between faith and life. This stage can be the most critical stage, the most difficult, the most complex.

6. Discovery of Commitment

Young people at this stage widen their horizons to another dimension of life: commitment. It is the moment of saying "yes" to the Lord's call: "Come, follow me" (Mt 19:21) and "Go to all parts of the world and announce the good news to all creatures" (Mk 16:16). There is an important difference here. In previous stages young people would oscillate between bursts of enthusiasm, when taking on certain tasks, followed by moments of discouragement and irresponsibility. However now the young people have been molded into leaders. They are persevering. Adverse circumstances are incapable of deterring them. Commitment no longer depends on feelings of the moment. They have now embraced a life style that is permanent.

7. Discovery of Previous Stages

This last stage is the phase of pedagogical maturity. Youth leaders are now more realistic. They are aware of the gradual character of growth toward faith maturity and commitment and of the patience needed to deal with it. "Effective educators accept people where they are and then help them move from there by stimulating understanding and growth" (Hill, 1988). They avoid imposing their views and demanding the same level of commitment from beginners. Youth leaders can distinguish the stages of the young people they work with, respect these stages and help the more courageous to face the challenge of new stages. Care is taken not to confuse the desired-level-of-commitment with the possible-level-of-commitment. Leaders realize that the process of education in the faith is slow and different for each person.

Notes

[1] Inaugural discourse of John Paul II in Santo Domingo (São Paulo: St. Paul Press, 1993), p. 39.

[2] Michael Warren, *Youth and the Future of the Church* (Minneapolis: The Seabury Press, 1982).

[3] I am following the ideas here of two authors, John Westerhoff and James Fowler, who gave important contributions to the development model of stages of faith. Later in this book we will study some of the ideas of Fowler. Cf. James Fowler, *Stages of Faith: The Psychology of Human Development and the Quest for Meaning* (San Francisco: Harper & Row, 1981), and John Westerhoff, Will Our Children Have Faith? (New York: Seabury Press, 1976).

[4] Cf. John Westerhoff, *Will Our Children Have Faith?* (New York: Seabury Press, 1976).

[5] *Hope for the Decade: A Look at the Issues Facing Catholic Youth Ministry* (Washington, D.C.: U.S. Catholic Conference, 1980).

[6] A summary of this model appears in the book entitled *Pastoral da Juventude, Sim À Civilização do Amor* [Youth Ministry: Yes to a Civilization of Love], CELAM (Latin American Bishops' Conference) (São Paulo: Edições Paulinas). As a member of the Latin American writing committee responsible for elaborating the final document, I had the task of writing on this model.

[7] Valentin de Pablo, *Juventud, Iglesia y Comunidad* [Youth, Church and Community] (Madrid: CCS, 1985).

[8] Jesus Andrés Velas and Alejandro Londoño, *Grupos Juveniles* (Bogotá: Indo-American Press Service, 1981).

[9] Carmen María Cervantes (ed.), *Hispanic Young People and the Church's Pastoral Response* (Winona: Saint Mary's Press, 1994), p. 213.

[10] Eduardo Mercieca, Manena Barros, Tony Mifsud and Osvaldo Almarza, *Proceso Grupal* [Group Process] (Bogotá: Indo-American Press Service, 1981).

[11] Ibid.

[12] Valentin de Pablo, *Juventud, Iglesia y Comunidad* [Youth, Church and Community] (Madrid: CCS, 1985).

[13] Michael Warren, *Youth and the Future of the Church* (Minneapolis: The Seabury Press, 1982).

[14] Parker J. Palmer, *The Promise of Paradox* (Notre Dame: Ave Maria Press, 1990).

[15] Since the classical work of Avery Dulles, S.J. on models of church, many other authors have presented theories which explain different models present in the church today. Authors present criteria for distinguishing models which are more authentic and others which are the result of cultural influences throughout history.

[16] Cf. Latin American bishop's document at Medellín, *A Igreja na Atual Transformação da América Latina À Luz do Concílio* (Petrópolis: Editora Vozes, 1971).

[17] Cf. Vatican II, (Evangelii nuntrandi Decree on the Apostolate of the Laity, n. 12), and 72.

[18] Congregation for the Doctrine of the Faith, *Instruction on Christian Freedom and Liberation*, n. 74 (London: Truth Society, 1986).

[19] Draft of a pastoral letter to be completed in November of 1995 by leaders of Germany's Protestant and Catholic churches. The docment is modeled after a 1986 pastoral letter by U.S. Catholic bishops on the American economy and is significant because of its ecumenical origins.

[20] Michael Warren, *Youth and the Future of the Church* (Minneapolis: The Seabury Press, 1982).

[21] NCCB, *Economic Justice for All* (Washington, DC: USCC, 1986), no. 16.

[22] The Irish Episcopal Conference. *Work Is the Key: Toward an Economy That Needs Everyone* (Dublin: Veritas, 1992), p. 42.

[23] Albert Nolan, *Taking Sides* (London: Catholic Institute for International Relations [CIIR] and Catholic Truth Society [CTS]).

[24] The method of active-non-violence is an alternative to armed struggle. It was used with great efficacy by Gandhi, the liberator of India. The method aims at overcoming the enemy by the force of superior moral values. Pressure that comes from the organization and conscientization of the people is also important. The method must not be confused with passivity. A strike, a march, a political gathering, a boycott, a hunger strike, campaign of protest letters, and campaigns to elect suitable candidates in an election are some examples of non-violent strategies.

[25] Brennan R. Hill, *Key Dimensions of Religious Education* (Winona: Saint Mary's Press, 1988), p. 129.

[26] Cf. Scott Peck, *The Road Less Traveled* (New York: Touchstone Book, 1979), p. 95.

27 Anne Hope and Sally Timmel, *Training for Transformations* (South Africa: Mambo Press, 1984), p. 40.

28 *L'Osservatore Romano*, April 12, 1987, p. 4.

29 "Among these social realities, we must give special emphasis to political activity. This embraces a vast field, from the action of voting, passing through the involvement and leadership in some political party, to the exercise of public posts on different levels" (Puebla Document, no. 791).

30 Brennan Hill, *Key Dimensions of Religious Education* (Winona: St. Mary's Press, 1988).

31 *Medios de Acción* (Bogotá: J.T.C.).

32 The Santo Domingo document (1993) reconfirms the importance of the see-judge-act method as the principal method of formation of young people (cf. no. 119).

33 John Roberto, *Hope for the Decade* (Washington, D.C.: National CYO Federation, 1980).

34 Carol Gilligan in her book *In a Different Voice* argues that women are likely to approach moral problems from a caring orientation rather than the justice orientation proposed by Kohlberg. Her thesis would seem to complement rather than substitute Kohlberg's original theory.

35 Lawrence Kohlberg, *The Cognitive-Developmental Approach to Moral Education*, Readings in Moral Development, (Minneapolis: Winston Press, 1978), p. 50.

36 Cf. Newman and Newman, *An Introduction to the Psychology of Adolescents* (Homewood: Dorsey Press, 1979).

37 James Fowler, *Stages of Faith* (San Francisco: Harper & Row, 1976).

38 Ibid.

39 Cf. Newman and Newman, (1979). *Development Through Life: A Psychosocial Approach*, Homewood, IL: the Dorsey Press.

40 Cf. Lawrence Kohlberg, *The Cognitive-Developmental Approach to Moral Education: Readings in Moral Development* (Minneapolis: Winston Press, 1978), p. 50.

41 James Fowler, *Stages of Faith: The Psychology of Human Development and the Quest for Meaning* (San Francisco: Harper & Row, 1981).

42 John Walsh, *Evangelization and Justice* (New York: Orbis, 1982).